"This book will be a vital companion for anyone stru  offers hope and a solid, evidence-based pathway throu writes from the heart with a wonderful balance of wi ing key processes from the latest behavioral science in tical tools. You'll learn how to embrace your pain with ᴄ......ᴄ ᴀnd compassion, and how to live well and thrive in the face of adversity. I cannot recommend this book enough and I will be encouraging my clients, relatives, and friends to get a copy."

> —**Mike Sinclair, DPSych**, clinical director at City Psychology Group, and coauthor of *Mindfulness for Busy People*, *The Little ACT Workbook*, *The Little Depression Workbook*, and *The Little Anxiety Workbook*

"Russ Harris is a master of helping us apply the life-changing power of acceptance and commitment therapy (ACT) in our day-to-day lives, and *When Life Hits Hard* is no exception. This clear, well-written, and timely book gently guides us to a deep understanding of how to work effectively with life's most difficult experiences. Lots of us are struggling right now. Filled with clear explanations, real-world vignettes, and pragmatic suggestions, this book will *help*."

> —**Russell Kolts, PhD**, professor at Eastern Washington University, and author of *CFT Made Simple* and *The Compassionate-Mind Guide to Managing Your Anger*

"This book is a true gem. Not only is it packed with practical and manageable suggestions on how to cope with crisis, loss, and grief; it takes you through an easy-to-read, at times deeply personal, down-to-earth, compassionate, and loving journey too. Read this book. You are going to need it when life hits hard."

> —**Rikke Kjelgaard**, psychologist, author, and ACT trainer

"*When Life Hits Hard* is a lovely book for clients and clinicians alike. Harris's writing voice conveys deep empathy and compassion for the universal pain and suffering that comes with being human, and offers simple, patient, and practical tools to help guide the reader along in whatever difficult journey he or she may be travelling."

> —**Susan M. McCurry, PhD**, author of *When a Family Member Has Dementia*, and research professor at the University of Washington School of Nursing

"Personal and practical, *When Life Hits Hard* offers concrete, science-based strategies to help you navigate life's most turbulent waters—and does so in a way that is approachable and heartfelt. Reading it is like getting advice from your wisest, most down-to-earth friend if that friend also happened to have a PhD in coping with grief and loss. While nothing may be able to prepare us for life's most painful losses and identity-shattering events, there are things that can help guide us through the aftermath—this book is definitely one of them."

—**Jenna LeJeune, PhD**, licensed psychologist, affiliate faculty at Oregon Health and Sciences University, and coauthor of *Values in Therapy*

"It's a difficult thing to communicate complex ideas in a way that people can easily understand and relate to. It's particularly difficult when addressing a subject as significant as grief and loss. Russ Harris is an author who has this ability in spades, and he covers how to manage some of the most painful experiences we can have in his usual accessible style. This book is refreshingly honest and validating about the pain of loss, as well as being very useful in offering an evidence-based set of tools for charting a way through that pain."

—**Richard Bennett, ClinPsyD**, clinical psychologist, lecturer in the Centre for Applied Psychology at the University of Birmingham, and coauthor of *Acceptance and Commitment Therapy* and *The Mindfulness and Acceptance Workbook for Self-Esteem*

"*When Life Hits Hard* is a vital resource—a practical book for those who wish to rebuild a meaningful life after devastating loss, illuminated by Russ's warm and friendly voice. First, Russ will show you how to gradually learn to deal more effectively with loss in a way that is as effective as it is counterintuitive: unhooking from unhelpful thoughts and making kind space for painful emotions. Next, Russ will show you how to rebuild a valued life—a life richer in depth and meaning—which stands as a living monument to what most matters to you and yours."

—**Benjamin Schoendorff, MA, MSc**, director of the Contextual Psychology Institute in Montreal, QC, Canada; coeditor of *The ACT Matrix*; and coauthor of *The ACT Practitioner's Guide to the Science of Compassion*

When Life Hits Hard

How to Transcend Grief, Crisis, and Loss *with* Acceptance and Commitment Therapy

Russ Harris

New Harbinger Publications, Inc.

Publisher's Note

This publication is designed to provide accurate and authoritative information in regard to the subject matter covered. It is sold with the understanding that the publisher is not engaged in rendering psychological, financial, legal, or other professional services. If expert assistance or counseling is needed, the services of a competent professional should be sought.

NEW HARBINGER PUBLICATIONS is a registered trademark of New Harbinger Publications, Inc.

Distributed in Canada by Raincoast Books

Cover design by Amy Shoup

Acquired by Tesilya Hanauer

Edited by Jean Blomquist

Library of Congress Cataloging-in-Publication Data

Names: Harris, Russ, 1966- author.
Title: When life hits hard : how to transcend grief, crisis, and loss with acceptance
    and commitment therapy / Russ Harris.
Description: Oakland : New Harbinger Publications, 2021.
Identifiers: LCCN 2021005093 | ISBN 9781684039012 (trade paperback)
Subjects: LCSH: Grief. | Loss (Psychology) | Acceptance and commitment therapy.
Classification: LCC BF575.G7 H3727 2021 | DDC 155.9/37--dc23
LC record available at https://lccn.loc.gov/2021005093

Printed in the United States of America

23   22   21

10   9   8   7   6   5   4   3   2   1   First Printing

To my only child. When I wrote the original Australian version of this book, you were only five years old; and now, as I write this new version, you are a young man of fourteen. You have been, by far, my greatest teacher. Thank you for teaching me so much about living and loving, for helping me to grow and develop, for bringing so much joy and love into my life. I love you more than words can ever express.

Contents

Part 1: Regroup

Part 2: Rebuild

Part 3: Revitalize

Appendices

PART ONE

Regroup

1   When Life Hurts

Nothing prepares us for those huge and painful losses that tear our world apart: the death of a loved one; the loss of our health and independence through illness or injury; the loss of an intimate relationship through divorce, separation, or breakup; the loss of employment—and with it, status and wealth. And there's the loss of security, confidence, or well-being that usually follows our primary loss. Sometimes we experience several losses at once, especially when we experience life-shattering events such as violent crime, freak accidents, unexpected death, bankruptcy, warfare, fire, flood, earthquake, pandemic, and so on. We all fear such losses and try to avoid them, but sooner or later, if we live long enough, we all have them.

And one thing's for sure: the bigger the loss, the greater our pain. Depending on the nature and extent of our loss, we may experience shock, sadness, anger, fear, anxiety, dread, guilt, shame—perhaps even hatred, despair, or disgust. Sometimes the pain is so intense, so unbearable, that our nervous system takes over, switches off our feelings, and leaves us feeling numb, empty, or dead inside.

We often recover fairly quickly from minor losses, but major loss usually results in a crisis: a time of intense difficulty and uncertainty when we're dealing with something awful over which we have little control. (This is especially likely with those life-crushing, soul-destroying events that psychologists refer to as "trauma.") At the same time, or very soon thereafter, comes grief. Contrary to popular belief, grief is *not* sadness; it's not an emotion at all. *Grief* is a psychological process of reacting to any significant loss. When we grieve, we may feel emotions ranging from sadness and anxiety to anger and guilt, as well as physical reactions such as sleep distur-bance, fatigue, lethargy, apathy, and changes in appetite.

The Five Stages of Grief

Dr. Elisabeth Kübler-Ross described the stages of grief as denial, anger, bar-gaining, depression, and acceptance. Although she was referring to death and dying, these stages apply to all types of loss. These stages are not dis-crete and well-defined, most people don't experience them all, and they don't occur in a fixed order. They tend to ebb and flow and blend into one another, and often they seem to end but then start again. Whatever your loss, you will experience at least some of these stages, so let's briefly discuss them.

Denial refers to a conscious or unconscious refusal or inability to acknowledge the reality of the situation. This could manifest as being unwilling to talk or think about it, pretending it's not happening, feeling a sense of being numb or "shut down," or experiencing a pervasive sense of unreality—feeling like it's all a bad dream.

In the *anger* stage, you might get angry with yourself, others, or life itself. And anger's close relatives—resentment, indignation, fury, outrage, or a strong sense of unfairness or injustice—frequently visit.

Bargaining means attempting to strike deals that alter reality—for example, asking God for a reprieve or asking a surgeon to guarantee an operation will be successful. It frequently involves wishful thinking and fan-tasizing about alternative realities: "If only this had happened" or "If only that hadn't happened."

The *depression* stage does not refer to the common clinical disorder known as depression. Instead, it refers to the emotions of sadness, sorrow, regret, fear, anxiety, and uncertainty, which are natural human reactions to major loss.

Finally, the *acceptance* stage refers to making peace with our new reality instead of struggling with or avoiding it. This frees us up to invest our energy in gradually rebuilding our life.

Fight, Flight, Freeze

Amid the chaos of a major loss, we'll all experience some unpleasant physical reactions—the well-known "fight or flight" response. And some of us will also experience the lesser known "freeze" response.

To understand these responses, why they happen, and how they affect us, let's journey back in time. Imagine one of our ancient ancestors is hunting rabbits alone when suddenly he comes face to face with a huge mother bear. For a split second, he freezes. The mother bear is fiercely protective of the two young cubs by her side; she sees the human as a threat—and she charges.

To survive, our ancestor has two options: take flight or stay and fight. So, in a split second, his autonomic nervous system takes over. As you know, "autonomy" means making your own decisions. And that's how the autonomic nervous system gets its name: it makes its own decisions about what's good for you, without any input from your conscious mind. So your mind doesn't ask, *Should I fight or flee?* Your autonomic nervous system decides for you before you can even think, and it instantly revs up your body for fight or flight.

So back to our ancient ancestor: Fight-or-flight mode kicks in. Large muscles in his arms and legs, chest and neck, tense up, ready for action. His body floods with adrenaline and his heart races, pumping blood to his muscles. Now in fight mode, he throws his spear as hard as possible.

But he throws poorly. The spear just grazes the bear and barely draws blood. The bear is furious, and our ancestor has no other weapons. Nothing matters now except escape, so he runs away as fast as he possibly can. But the mother bear is faster. She catches him and knocks him to the ground.

He can't fight off the bear, and he can't run away. So again, his autonomic nervous system instantly takes control. Recognizing that fight or flight is no longer useful, the nervous system switches the body over to "freeze." Why? Because bears don't like their prey fighting back. So the more the man screams and struggles, the more viciously the bear will attack him. His best chance of survival is to lie still and be as quiet as possible.

In the freeze response, the vagus nerve (the second-largest nerve in the body, after the spinal cord) actively immobilizes the man: it paralyzes his muscles so he literally can't move. And at the same time, it shuts off his ability to physically feel. Why? Because the less pain he feels, the less he'll scream and struggle. So he lies there, literally "frozen stiff," "paralyzed by fright," "numb with fear." If he's lucky, when he falls silent and lies still, the bear might lose interest and go away—or he might survive long enough for someone to rescue him.

Our nervous systems and bodies are hard-wired to react in these ways— fight, flight, or freeze—to any type of threat. (We have this in common with the nervous systems of all other mammals, as well as birds, reptiles, and most types of fish.) All losses threaten us. They may threaten our health, our well-being, our lifestyle, our security, our happiness, and so on. And the greater the loss, the more threatening it is. So when significant losses occur, we'll all have a fight-or-flight response. Most commonly this manifests as fear and anxiety (flight), but sometimes anger will predominate (fight). And in the most severe cases, if our nervous system perceives that fight or flight is futile, we'll go into freeze mode, literally freezing up, unable to move or speak. We may even black out or have an out-of-body experience.

In the days and weeks following a major loss, fight, flight, or freeze responses are likely to arise again and again. They are triggered by anything that reminds us of what we've been through, including both things inside us—such as memories, thoughts, feelings, and sensations—and things outside us, such as certain people, places, food, music, photographs, objects, books, news reports, and so on. "Fight" shows up as anger, frustration, and irritability, "flight" as fear, anxiety, and worry, and "freeze" as numbness, apathy, tiredness, zoning out, or disengaging, which often feeds into a sense of futility, hopelessness, and despair.

Now that we've touched on common reactions to loss, the big question is, What can we do about our reactions?

What Can We Do?

The truth is, most of us don't cope well with loss. We're easily hooked by those painful thoughts, feelings, memories, and physical reactions; they jerk us around and pull us into self-defeating behaviors. For example, we might overuse drugs and alcohol, withdraw from our friends and family, drop out of activities we used to enjoy, fight with the people we love, hide away from the world, or spend too much time in bed and on the couch.

All of these behaviors are normal—and extremely common. The problem is that they usually make things worse rather than better. But here's the good news: we can change this state of affairs; we can learn new and more effective ways of responding to grief, loss, and crisis. This book is based on an approach called acceptance and commitment therapy, or ACT (pronounced as the word "act," not as the initials). ACT is a science-based approach, created by psychologist Steven C. Hayes back in the 1980s. At the time of writing (2020), more than three thousand studies on ACT have been published in top scientific journals and demonstrate its effectiveness with everything from grief, depression, and anxiety to addiction, chronic illness, and trauma. It's a powerful and practical approach that helps people transcend their pain and suffering, and build rich, meaningful lives despite adversity. And in the chapters that follow, I'll take you through it gently, step by step.

However, before we go any further, I really need to emphasize two points. First, there is no single "right" or "appropriate" reaction to a major loss. Everyone reacts differently, so please let go of any preconceived ideas about what you should or shouldn't feel, and how long it should or shouldn't last. For example, some people cry for days and weeks on end, while others never shed a single tear; both reactions are normal. Second, there is no single "best" or "correct" way to cope with grief, loss, and crisis. Everyone copes differently, and what works for one person may not work for another. This book gives you lots of tips, tools, strategies, and suggestions that have proven to be helpful for many people—but nothing works for everyone. So please, experiment, modify, and adapt everything in this book to make it work for your unique situation and the challenges that go with it. (And that means dropping anything that *doesn't* work!)

By the time most people get to my age (53), they have experienced a fair number of losses. My first big losses occurred in childhood, as a result of repeated abuse from two close relatives. In later life, my losses included the deaths of both parents, deaths of friends and other family members, a painful divorce, a major injury resulting in chronic pain, and an intensely stressful period of four years when my young son needed intensive ongoing treatment for a very serious condition. (To my great relief, he eventually made a full recovery. We were extremely fortunate; I know many people reading this book are not so lucky.) I've found ACT enormously helpful in dealing with these difficult events in my own life, and I've also used it to help many others.

What's impressed me most about the ACT model is its universal applicability. In 2015, I wrote an ACT program for the World Health Organization (WHO) for use in refugee camps. WHO has now used this program to good effect in many different countries, including Turkey, Uganda, and Syria. The people in these camps have suffered multiple huge losses due to warfare, persecution, violence, and having to exchange their beloved homes and countries for the bleak living conditions of a refugee camp. I must confess that I was initially doubtful about the program: I wondered how it could possibly help people facing such great adversity. Because of my concerns, I was both relieved and delighted when WHO finally published its research several years later: the refugees not only liked the program, but they also found it very helpful for coping with their harsh life circumstances.

The book you're reading is very similar to the WHO program. I've divided it into three sections. Part 1 is titled Regroup, which means to reorganize after a setback and regain your composure. Our main focus here is how to take care of yourself and deal with all those painful thoughts and feelings. Part 2, Rebuild, explores how to rebuild your life, one small step at a time—no matter how extensive and severe the wreckage may be. Part 3, Revitalize, focuses on how to bring back your vigor and vitality, and to appreciate what life still has to offer. To supplement this book, I've created a free e-book called *When Life Hits Hard: Extra Bits*. It contains additional resources, mostly free audio recordings of the exercises in this book. You can get the e-book from the Free Resources page on my website, www .thehappinesstrap.com.

At this point, your mind may protest; it might insist that your case is different, this book won't help, and your life will remain empty or unbearable. If so, rest assured: those are perfectly natural thoughts that many people have when they're new to this approach. And the fact is, even though this book is very likely to help you, I can't actually *guarantee* it. However, here's what I *can* guarantee: I guarantee that if you stop reading now because your mind has doubts, then you definitely *won't* get any benefit from this book!

So if your mind is casting doubt, how about we just let it have its say? Let it tell you whatever it wants, but don't let that stop you from reading. Let your mind chatter away like a radio playing in the background, and together let's explore how to survive and thrive when life hits hard.

2 First Things First

Natalie's face was as pale as a winter moon. Tears streamed down her cheeks and splashed on her blouse, and her whole body shook as she cried. Ten days earlier, her teenage son had been struck and instantly killed by a hit-and-run driver. The police had still not found the offender. "My heart has broken into a million pieces," Natalie sobbed. "What can I do? What can I do?" she kept saying. "I don't know what to do."

Focus on What's in Your Control

When loss or trauma tears a gaping hole in our universe, most of us feel powerless as we struggle to come to terms with terrible events over which we have little or no control. So, in this chapter, we'll look at some practical tips for dealing with the immediate aftermath of a loss.

Let's begin by acknowledging that fear and anxiety are inevitable; they are normal responses to life-disrupting situations infused with threat and uncertainty. We start worrying about all sorts of things that are out of our control: what might happen in the future, how this might affect us or our loved ones, what will happen then, and so on. It's also easy to dwell on the past: reliving painful events, wondering what we could have done differently, imagining how that might have changed what happened, trying to figure out just who or what was to blame. But the more we focus on what's not in our control, the more hopeless, anxious, or angry we're likely to feel. So the single most useful response to any type of loss, crisis, or trauma is to *focus on what's in your control.*

We can't control what happens in the future. We can't control what happened in the past. We can't control what other people do. And we definitely can't control our thoughts and feelings; we can't eliminate all those painful emotions and memories and somehow magically replace them with joy and happiness. But we *can* control what we *do*—we *can* control the physical actions we take. This is where we need to focus our energy and attention. This is the first step in surviving a big loss: take control of your actions. Let's explore some ways to do this.

No One Is an Island

When Shanti's husband left her and ran off with her childhood friend (with whom he'd been having an affair for two years), Shanti was, in her own words, "shattered." Her emotional storms included roaring floods of rage, torrential downpours of sadness, and gale-force winds of anxiety, shame, and embarrassment. Shanti reacted to her loss by hiding from the outside world. She cut off contact with friends and family, and locked herself inside her house. Michelle did something very similar, following a violent sexual assault. So did Dave, after he lost his job. Shanti, Michelle, and Dave all had similar motivations for their isolation. They didn't want to see other people because they didn't want to talk about what had happened. They were afraid it would be too awkward, too uncomfortable, and that it would bring up too many painful feelings and memories.

With Helen and Philip, the motivation for withdrawal was somewhat different. Helen's husband died suddenly and unexpectedly from a massive heart attack. Philip's husband died over several months from pancreatic cancer . Following these losses, Helen and Philip withdrew from friends and family mainly because they were exhausted; they just didn't have energy to cope with social interaction.

Sometimes we may withdraw from specific groups of people. This is most likely when they still have something we have lost. When we see the huge discrepancy between their life and ours, it can be too painful to bear. For example, after her baby girl died from meningitis, Yoko withdrew from all her friends who had children; Alana did the same after her miscarriage. For both of them, it was just too painful to be around families with young kids.

Rada's loss came in the form of a medical condition called fibromyalgia. She experienced intense painful burning and throbbing sensations in her upper arms, shoulders, neck, back, and abdomen, along with headaches, stiffness, and extreme fatigue. This severely limited her ability to do many of her once daily activities. So Rada withdrew from her loved ones because (a) it was so exhausting to socialize, and (b) it was so physically painful and tiring to get out of the house.

There are so many different reasons why we may retreat from those we are closest to. We might not want to burden or impose on others. Or others may be awkward and not know how to be with us or what to say to us—and, of course, that's uncomfortable for us as well as for them. Or we may get hooked by the stoic belief that "I should be able to get through this on my own; I don't need anyone else."

All of these reactions are completely normal and natural. (Yes, I've used that phrase quite a few times already, but it's important to repeat this message, because we are so quick to judge our reactions as abnormal, defective, or wrong.) The problem is, when we withdraw from others, it usually amplifies our suffering. You've probably heard the phrase "humans are social animals." If we wish to thrive, we need quality time with others. Yet all too often, when life slaps us around, we pull away from the people who care about us most. And cocooned in our misery, cut off from loved ones, our pain only increases.

So it's important that we reach out to others who are caring, supportive, and understanding. Who can you connect with? And how might you connect with them—face to face, phone calls, video chats, text messages? Reaching out to others is something that's in our control. It is fine, of course, to set limits on how much time you spend together and what you do: "Just called to touch base; I can only chat for five minutes," "Yes, sure—please do drop by, but thirty minutes is probably all I can cope with right now," "If it's okay with you, I don't really want to talk about what happened," "I don't want to talk, I just want you to hold me," "Let's just watch a movie."

It's also fine to say no. If you're genuinely not up to being with others, honor that. Likewise, if you are interacting with others and you feel you need a break, it's fine to leave. Just say, "I'm sorry, I need a break. I'm a bit overwhelmed right now." Then go for a walk or retire to another room.

Unfortunately, one issue we often encounter is that other people don't have a clue how to treat us; they try to help, but all too often it falls flat. They may offer us platitudes—"Everything happens for a reason"—push us to think "positively" or "rationally," or tell us to "Be strong!" Or they may avoid asking us about what happened and how we're feeling, and try instead to distract us and change the topic. Or they may talk about how things will be so much better in the future, give us advice on how to fix our problems, or get preachy: "God only gives us what we can handle." And it's not their fault; they're usually trying their best to help and support us. Unfortunately, the society we live in doesn't teach us how to do this well.

Experiment to Find Out What Works

A quick Google search will reveal a vast electronic warehouse of advice on how to cope with your loss. Some of it's very good, and some is absolute rubbish—and nothing you find there will hold true for everyone. So we really need to experiment, to try different things and find out what works for us.

With that caution in mind, I will share two practical tips. First, many people find it helpful to get outside. Walks in nature are often quite comforting. They give both a sense of connection with something bigger than us and the relief of escape from the challenges of life indoors. In nature, it's easy to be yourself; you don't have to put on a brave face for the grass, the trees, and the sky. You don't have to do anything at all. You can walk, breathe, and notice the world around you, and let yourself feel whatever you're feeling.

Second, be wary of making big decisions. It's hard to make big decisions at the best of times—and it's doubly difficult following a huge loss. We're often exhausted or sleep deprived; our minds are grappling with so many different things that we find it hard to think straight. So if you do have big decisions to make, ask yourself these questions: Can I postpone these decisions for a while? Can I delegate them to someone I trust? If those aren't options for you, at the very least use the "dropping anchor" practice in chapter 5 to ground and center you before making that decision.

Many popular ideas about how to cope with grief, loss, and trauma appeal to common sense but have no scientific validity. One of these is the notion that you have to express your feelings. Well, the fact is, you don't. For sure, *most* people find it's helpful to express their feelings—and if you think or know that this would be helpful for you, there are many ways to do it. The simplest way is to talk honestly and openly about your feelings to friends, family, a support group, or a therapist. A very popular alternative is to write about your feelings in a journal. If you're creative, you might prefer to express your feelings in the form of poetry, prose, music, painting, drawing, sculpting, or even dance.

However, it's important to know that not everyone finds it helpful to do this, and it's definitely *not* essential! You can survive and thrive in the face of your loss without ever talking or writing about your feelings. So if you're not sure that expressing your feelings is for you, arguably the best option is to experiment with it and observe what happens. If you find it helpful, keep doing it; if not, stop.

Self-Care: A Balancing Act

The term "self-care" might make you roll your eyeballs and groan. But we do need to talk about it. Of course, right now, even the thought of "self-care" may overwhelm you. If so, that's okay. Over the next few chapters, you'll learn how to handle that sense of being overwhelmed and gently motivate yourself to do what's important for you.

Self-care is a bit of a balancing act. On the one hand, we want to give ourselves a break—take the pressure off ourselves, drop some of our respon-sibilities, take time to rest up and recuperate. On the other hand, we want to keep doing things that are healthy for us. So, for example, many of us will benefit from increased rest and downtime following a major loss. This makes sense because shocking life events eat up a lot of energy, emotional storms are exhausting, and often our sleep is disrupted. However, if we go to the extreme of staying in bed or lying on the couch for large parts of the day or for weeks on end—well, that's likely to make us worse in the long run, not better.

Likewise, many people turn to comfort eating—chocolate, ice cream, pizza—or drinking more alcohol than usual. In moderation, alcohol use isn't likely to be an issue, but if we drink excessively, it adds more problems to those we already have.

Same deal with exercise: it's normal for our exercise routines to drop off, given the stress and strain we're going through. But if we give up all exercise, our health will suffer, so it's important to keep the body moving. This is especially true if you have a chronic illness or injury, like Rada. Because of all the pain, stiffness, and exhaustion she experienced with her fibromyalgia, Rada simply couldn't do the physical activities she'd previously enjoyed, especially Latin dancing and aerobics. But without any physical exercise at all, fibromyalgia gets worse over time, and so does almost any chronic illness you can think of—from diabetes to heart disease, from asthma to hypertension. This meant that Rada had to find new ways of exercising within the limitations imposed by her illness. Initially, this involved basic stretching and strengthening exercises assigned by her physical therapist, and taking extremely short walks assisted by a walking stick.

It's worth spending a bit of time on creating a self-care plan. Consider how you can care for yourself physically through exercise, healthy eating, moderating any drug and alcohol use, appropriate rest and relaxation, and sensible sleep routines. At the same time, be realistic: if this all seems too hard—too much, too soon, too overwhelming—then it's okay to leave it for now. By the time you get to chapter 18, Breaking Bad Habits, you'll have all the tools you need to effectively motivate yourself.

And don't forget about hobbies, sports, creative pursuits, and other interests. These are often abandoned during times of upheaval. Sometimes it's wise to put these activities on the back burner for a while, as you focus on dealing with your problems. However, for many people, the sooner they can get back to these activities, the better. You might not initially enjoy them as much as you used to; you might be too emotional, tired, or drained to engage in them fully. But if you persist, you may be surprised at how they comfort, encourage, or sustain you amid your suffering.

Obviously, you need to adapt self-care to suit your unique circumstances. If you're recovering from major surgery, chemotherapy, or a serious illness, you won't be able to work out at the gym, but you may be able to do gentle exercises in bed. And once you're able to get out of bed, you can gradually build up your strength over time with simple exercises your doctor can recommend. If your loss doesn't involve injury or illness, you'll obviously have many more exercise options, but you might not have the energy to do your usual routines. In that case, give yourself permission to do something easier, like going for a walk.

When Natalie kept repeating, "What can I do?" she was asking a valuable question. There was nothing she could do to change the past, to bring her son back, to heal her fragmented heart. However, she could do tiny little acts of self-care—an important step in regaining a semblance of control over her life.

Remember: self-care doesn't have to involve great effort. Every time you brush your teeth, take a shower, eat something healthy—that's self-care. So is reaching out to friends, listening to music you love, or reading this book. And every little bit of self-care counts (even if your mind says it doesn't).

3   Kind Words

When life hits hard and leaves you reeling, what do you want most from those closest to you? Most of us want to know someone is there for us—someone who truly cares about us, who takes time to understand us, who recognizes our pain and appreciates how badly we are suffering; who allows us to share our true feelings without expecting us to cheer up, put on a brave face, or pretend everything is okay; who supports us, treats us kindly, and offers to help; who demonstrates through their actions that we are not alone. So, if we'd like others to treat us with caring, understanding, and kindness, why do most of us treat *ourselves* so badly?

We need all the kindness we can get, yet we often find it difficult to access. Why? Because our minds naturally tend to judge, criticize, and beat us up; to pull out a big stick and give us a beating; to kick us when we're already down. Our minds may tell us we're not being strong enough, we should be handling things better, or others are far worse off than we are, so we have nothing to complain about. They may tell us to get a grip, sort ourselves out, or stop being weak or pathetic. Sometimes our minds may even say that we are to blame for our loss.

When someone we love dies, the mind might blame us for not loving them enough, or not being there enough, or not telling them enough how much we loved them, and sometimes even for not preventing their death (especially common in cases of suicide)! One client blamed himself for surviving a plane crash. His mind told him it wasn't fair that he survived when twelve other passengers died—that he didn't deserve to live. (This is known as "survivor guilt.") Another client blamed herself for her son's schizophrenia: "It was my fault; I gave him bad genes."

Even if it doesn't attack us personally, the mind is often callous, cold, and uncaring: it crushes our spirit, tells us we can't cope, that life's not worth living, that we should stop moaning, whining, complaining—or it may conjure up terrible fears about what's to come. As I keep saying, this is normal, but it's not particularly helpful. So what's the alternative?

Hippy Shit!

Antonio grimaced. A huge, muscle-bound cop, he crossed his arms tightly across his chest. "Don't give me that hippy shit!" he growled. Antonio's wife, Cathy, had pushed him to see me, and he resented it. Several weeks earlier, Antonio's baby, Sophia, had died from sudden infant death syndrome (SIDS). He and Cathy were devastated, but they both were handling their grief differently.

Cathy was doing many of the things we discussed in chapter 2: reaching out to friends and family, expressing her feelings, allowing herself to cry (sometimes for hours on end), and mostly taking good care of herself. In stark contrast, Antonio was cutting himself off from just about everyone and spending every evening in front of the TV, saying little but drinking heavily. Whenever Cathy tried to talk to him about their loss, their heartache, their suffering, Antonio would get angry and shut her down.

Despite his resentment at seeing me, Antonio cared deeply about Cathy and wanted to make things better. He saw quickly that his behavior was largely an attempt to escape pain. He loved his work, and during the day he threw himself into it and mostly forgot about his loss. But not at home. Everything there reminded him of baby Sophia, especially his wife. And with those reminders came pain like he'd never known. Drinking, refusing to talk, zoning out in front of the TV: these behaviors gave him some relief from that terrible pain—but at a huge cost to his relationship with his wife.

"I'm a fucking asshole," he said. "I should be there for her, but I'm not. It's just, it's just...I just don't fucking want to think about it. It's too, it's just too...ah, I'm so fucking weak. I'm pathetic."

"You're pretty good at beating yourself up," I said.

"Yeah, well, I fucking deserve it, don't I?"

"And is all that beating yourself up helping you to deal with the situation?"

"What do you think?" he asked sarcastically. "Of course it fucking isn't."

"So," I said, "given it's not really helping, are you open to trying something different?"

Antonio looked at me suspiciously. "Like what?"

"Like actually being kind to yourself."

"Don't give me that hippy shit!" he growled.

Antonio's reaction was common. Many people initially resist the idea of self-kindness. "What's hippy-ish about it?" I asked.

"I know what you're up to," he said. "Cathy's been banging on about this for days, this whatchamacallit?—self-compassion. You're seriously gonna try and sell that shit to me?"

I took a deep breath. "If I ask you a question, will you give me an honest answer?"

He shrugged. "Sure."

"Okay. Let's suppose you're traveling with a friend. It's a tough and dangerous journey, and all sorts of terrible things keep happening. You're really struggling to keep going."

Antonio shifted uncomfortably in his chair.

"Now," I went on, "as you continue the journey, what kind of friend do you want with you—a friend who says, 'Ah, shut up! Stop your whining.

Stop being such a wimp. Suck it up and get on with it, you big sissy!'? Or do you want a friend who says, 'This is really shit. But hey, we're in this together. I've got your back, and I'm with you every step of the way.'"

Antonio cleared his throat. "Well, obviously the second one," he said.

"So what kind of friend are you being to yourself?" I asked. "Are you like the first or the second?"

What Is Self-Compassion?

There are many definitions of *self-compassion*, and they all boil down to this: acknowledge your pain, respond with kindness. Those six simple words summarize a wealth of wisdom. Self-compassion means recognizing that you're in pain and then doing something kind, caring, and supportive to help ease your suffering.

If we can learn how to treat ourselves kindly, we'll be much better at handling our pain and dealing with all those problems life just dumped on us. Yet many people initially dismiss self-compassion. They may think it's flowery, airy-fairy, New Age, hippy-ish, or touchy-feely. Some see it as psychobabble without any scientific validity. Others perceive it as a religious practice. Men may see it as "effeminate" or "unmanly." And gender aside, many people see it as "weak," "soft," or "not really dealing with your problems."

But none of these are valid criticisms. Yes, there are religious practices for self-compassion, and over the years, the merits of self-compassion have often been touted by hippies and New Agers. But times change. Self-compassion is now firmly in the domain of Western science. Many respected scientists have researched the benefits of self-compassion (without any religious element to it) and found it to be helpful with a wide range of problems, from anxiety and depression to grief and trauma.

There's nothing weak or unmanly about being kind to a friend who's in great pain, so shouldn't the same be true when we're kind to ourselves? And the research tells us that self-compassion actually helps us deal with our problems; it helps us regroup and recharge so we have the motivation and energy to take effective action.

Sometimes people confuse self-compassion with self-pity. "What's the use of feeling sorry for yourself?" they ask. But self-pity is the very opposite of self-compassion; it's an excessive absorption in your own troubles, wallowing in them without doing anything to help yourself. That's a far cry from the brief self-compassion strategies you'll learn in this book, where you quickly acknowledge your pain (without pity, without wallowing) and do something practical to relieve it.

I've had many clients who've opposed self-compassion, saying, "I don't have time for this; I have to take care of my family." I ask them, "Have you ever flown on an airplane? Remember that warning they give you: always put on your own oxygen mask first before giving assistance to others? That's because if you don't get your mask on within about thirty seconds, you'll pass out, and then you can't help anyone. So think of self-compassion as putting on your oxygen mask so you can cope much better and also take care of others." Sometimes, people misunderstand and think self-compassion means "giving up" or "not dealing with your problems." Actually, self-compassion helps you to keep going *instead of* giving up, and it gives you the strength to actually deal with your problems.

Some people resist self-compassion because they think it's selfish or self-indulgent. But if your best friend was struggling through a really tough patch, wouldn't you support and help your friend through it? And if they accepted your help and kindness, would you judge them as self-indulgent or selfish? Of course you wouldn't. So why the double standard? If your friend deserves kindness and caring in their time of need, so do you.

Now notice what your mind says about that. Does it agree, or is it protesting, *No, you don't deserve it!?* If it's the latter, please know we've all got different versions of the "I'm Not Good Enough" story, and this variation—I'm Unworthy, I Don't Deserve Kindness—is extremely common. Later, we'll learn how to deal with "not good enough" stories, but, for now, please simply acknowledge that thought. Say to yourself, *Okay, here's my mind beating me up, criticizing me, telling me I don't deserve this.* After that, let your mind say whatever it wants. Don't argue with it, because you almost certainly won't win. Just let your mind do its "schtick," while you do the exercises later in this chapter.

Acknowledging Your Pain

"Okay, I get your point," said Antonio. "But I don't think I can do that sort of stuff. As a cop, you learn to suck it up."

I nodded. "Yes, your default setting is like the first friend: "Suck it up, get on with it, stop whining, no one cares!"

Antonio nodded. "That's pretty much it."

"But if your best friend's daughter had just died, that's not what you'd say to him, is it?"

"No, of course not!"

"What would you say to him?"

"Ah, Jesus! I wouldn't have a f###ing clue!"

"Well, just think about it. Usually when people are in great pain, they want to hear two things: (1) 'I can see you're hurting'; (2) 'I'm here for you.' So how would you say that in your own words?"

Antonio thought for a moment, then said softly, "I guess I'd say, 'This is really f###ing shit, man. It's the worst ever. It shouldn't happen to anyone. Especially not you. I'm here for ya…whatever you need…' At this point, his voice cracked. The tough cop mask disappeared, and tears welled in his eyes.

Like many of us, Antonio knew how to be compassionate to others but struggled to be compassionate with himself. If you don't relate to that struggle, you're very lucky. I'll assume that most readers—like me when I first learned about it—will find self-compassion quite challenging, so I'll introduce it in small steps. And the first step is simply to acknowledge our pain—because losses hurt. They hurt *so much*. And we so badly want that pain to stop, but all too often, it doesn't.

Kind self-talk has two main elements, both of which you can see in Antonio's imagined speech:

1. acknowledge your pain

2. respond with kindness

The First Step: Acknowledge Pain

Acknowledging our pain simply means being honest with ourselves about just how much this hurts—without dwelling on it, wallowing in it, or turning it into self-pity. So, for example, we wouldn't go into a long internal monologue: *This is awful. I can't bear it any longer. I've never felt so bad. When's it going to stop?* That's a recipe for misery and despair. We want to acknowledge our pain in a kind, honest way.

One way to do this is to create a short, easy-to-remember phrase that also helps us step back a little from our suffering. Phrases such as "Here is…," "I'm noticing…," "I'm having…" are particularly useful. For example, "Here is sadness," "I'm noticing anger," "I'm having feelings of despair." This is an odd way of speaking—and that's deliberate. You see, we often say things like "I am sad," "I am lonely," or "I am angry"—and that makes it seem as if *I am the emotion*. These unusual ways of speaking—"I'm noticing fear" or "Here is anxiety"— help us to stand slightly back from our pain, to detach from it a little, which makes it less likely to sweep us away. And if you can't pinpoint the exact feeling you're noticing, or if there are so many you can't distinguish them, you can use terms like "suffering," "grief," "hurt," "loss," "pain," or "heartbreak": "Here is suffering," "I'm noticing heartbreak." On the other hand, if your freeze response kicked in and cut off your feelings, you might say, "I'm noticing numbness" or "Here is a feeling of emptiness."

It can also help to include phrases such as "here and now" or "in this moment." If we say, "Here and now, I'm noticing loss," "In this moment, grief is here," or "Right here and now, I'm noticing anger," this reminds us of the transient nature of painful thoughts and feelings—just like the weather, they continually change. Even during the worst days of your life, your emotions will change; at times you'll feel better and at times you'll feel worse. So "here and now" you might be noticing sadness, but later you'll be noticing something else. Other phrases you could use include, "This is a moment of," or "This is an experience of." For example, "This is a moment of great sadness" or "This is an experience of anger."

Play around with these words and come up with a phrase that works for you. Kristin Neff, the world's top researcher on self-compassion, likes to say, "This is a moment of suffering." There's something poetic in this phrase that appeals to many people. However, some people prefer everyday language. For example, Rada, who was suffering from fibromyalgia, preferred to say, "This really hurts." And Natalie, whose son died in a hit-and-run accident, came up with, "I'm noticing heartbreak." As for Antonio, he preferred the simple phrase, "Here is…": "Here is sadness," "Here is anger," and so on.

I encourage you to try this now.

Acknowledge Your Pain

Take a moment to notice any difficult feelings that are present right now and label them: anger, sadness, anxiety, loneliness, and so on.

And then, very slowly, using a calm, kind, peaceful inner voice, acknowledge it: *I'm noticing...* or *Here is....*

Now pause for a moment, and take a slow and gentle breath, in and out.

And now, try this once more.

Very slowly, in a calm, kind, peaceful inner voice, acknowledge it: *I'm noticing...* or *Here is....*

The Second Step: Respond with Kindness

The next step, after we acknowledge our pain, is to remind ourselves to respond with kindness. So, for example, we might silently say, *Be kind to yourself, Go easy on yourself, Give yourself a break, Ease off,* or *Gently does it.* Some people prefer a single word like *Gentle* or *Kind.* Kristin Neff, the researcher I mentioned above, says, *May I be kind to myself.* Rada simply said, *Be kind.* Natalie chose *May I treat myself kindly.* Antonio, after quite a bit of struggle, chose *Go easy on yourself.*

The Final Step: Bringing Acknowledgment and Kindness Together

The final step brings acknowledging your pain and responding with kindness together. You combine them in a phrase you can use over and over:

This really hurts. Be kind.

I'm noticing heartbreak. May I treat myself kindly.

Here is sadness. Go easy on yourself.

This is a moment of suffering. May I be kind to myself.

Once you've done this, repeat these words to yourself, using a calm, kind, peaceful inner voice whenever you struggle with your pain. The aim is to give yourself a sense of comfort and support, as if you have a caring friend by your side.

Also, remember that this isn't a "positive thinking" practice; you're not banishing negative thoughts and replacing them with positive ones. If you use self-compassion for that purpose, you'll soon be disappointed. Harsh, unhelpful, or self-judgmental thoughts will continue to arise (later in the book, we'll discuss why). The aim here is to allow your thoughts and feelings to be as they are in this moment, while simultaneously bringing in kind self-talk. In other words, rather than trying to get rid of unwanted thoughts, you're acknowledging they are present, allowing them to stay, and adding some new ones to keep them company. (If this seems odd, it will make more sense after you've read the next two chapters.)

In a moment, I'll ask you to try this out: create your own phrase, or pick one of the four I listed above, and say it to yourself with genuine kindness—using a calm, soft, gentle inner voice.

But first, let me make a prediction. About 95 percent of readers will do the exercise that follows and get some immediate benefit. About 5 percent will have a negative reaction; either, disappointingly, nothing much will happen, or the exercise will bring up difficult thoughts and feelings (most likely anxiety, self-criticism, or some version of "I don't deserve it"). If you're in the 5 percent, rest assured that's not a problem, because over the next few chapters, you'll learn skills that will make this much easier. Okay, now let's try it!

Some Kind Words

Find a comfortable position in which you are centered and alert. For example, if you're seated in a chair, you could lean slightly forward, straighten your back, drop your shoulders, and press your feet gently into the floor.

Now bring to mind whatever you are struggling with. Take a few moments to reflect on what has happened, and how it affects you. Notice what difficult thoughts and feelings arise.

Then using a kind, calm inner voice, speaking to yourself slowly and softly, take a moment to genuinely acknowledge your pain and respond with kindness. If you're stuck for ideas, try "This really hurts. Be kind."

Now pause for a moment, and notice what happens.

And if you feel like it, take a breath—and ever so slowly and gently, allow the air to flow in and out of your lungs.

Now once again, repeat this phrase with kindness.

Then pause for a moment, and notice what happens.

And again, if you feel like it, take a breath: breathing in and out, slowly and gently.

Now, one last time, repeat those kind words to yourself, infusing them with warmth, care, and comfort.

And again, pause for a moment, and notice what happens.

So what happened? If nothing much happened, or if it brought up difficult thoughts and feelings, that's not a problem; I'm confident this will change as you work through the book. For now, just acknowledge that at this point in time, this type of kind self-talk is not working for you. The good news is, there are many other ways to treat yourself kindly. For example, consider those acts of self-care we discussed in chapter 2. If you do these things on autopilot, or out of a sense of compliance because your mind says, *You have to do this; you have to take care of yourself*, they're still useful, but they're unlikely to give you that sense of being kind to yourself. However, you can change that. Keep doing them but, as you do them, see if you can "sprinkle on" a sense of genuine warmth and caring. (You may not be able to do this, but give it a try.) Likewise, in the next few chapters, you'll learn a number of skills for handling your pain differently and reducing its impact. Each time you apply these skills to ease your suffering is an act of kindness in itself.

On the other hand, maybe this exercise *did* help you tap into a sense of self-kindness. Even if you only had the tiniest glimmer of it, that's a good start; self-compassion is a skill, and like any skill, it gets better with prac-tice. So, please play around with your kind self-talk until you find a phrase that resonates with you, and then repeat it to yourself throughout the day, especially in those moments when life hurts most. Notice what it's like when you turn toward yourself with genuine kindness, appreciate that sense of befriending yourself. When life hits you hard, self-kindness is your greatest ally.

4   Drop the Struggle

Shanti could barely look at me. Her voice was quiet and drenched with despair: "I just want to stop feeling this way!" You may recall Shanti from chapter 2. Her husband, Ravi, had been having an affair with Shanti's best friend for over two years. When Shanti found about it, Ravi left her and ran off with her friend. Shame, anger, betrayal, injustice, loneliness, sadness, and anxiety—these feelings and more kept showing up. Of course Shanti wanted to "stop feeling this way." None of us like pain; we all want it gone. But how much control do we really have over our feelings?

As infants, toddlers, and young children, we are largely controlled by our emotions. Fear, anger, sadness, guilt, frustration, and anxiety: these and many other emotions push children around as if they are remote-controlled robots. If anger shows up, they shout, yell, lash out, or stomp their feet. If fear shows up, they hide, cry, or run away. If sadness or disappointment shows up, they sulk or cry.

Fortunately, as adults we are much less controlled by our feelings, and this is a good thing. We'd be in big trouble if our feelings controlled us. Imagine if your fear, anger, sadness, and guilt pushed you around as it did when you were a child. How difficult would life be for you?

Yet, at times, we all get pushed around by our emotions. We may lose our temper, get carried away by our fears, find ourselves overwhelmed with sadness, get crushed with guilt, or go into a fit of blind rage. But fortunately, for most people, this happens much less than it did in childhood. Why? Because as we grew older, we learned different ways to control our feelings.

For example, we learned to distract ourselves from unpleasant emotions via food, music, TV, books, or games. And as we grew older, potential distractions multiplied: exercise, work, study, hobbies, religion, computer games, email, gambling, sex, pornography, music, sport, drugs, alcohol, gardening, walking the dog, cooking, dancing, and others. We also learned to escape unpleasant feelings by avoiding the situations where they were most likely to occur; in other words, we would withdraw or stay away from the people, places, activities, or tasks we found difficult or challenging.

We developed thinking strategies that could give us some relief from emotional pain. Most of us have a wealth of these strategies, such as these:

- doing constructive problem solving

- writing lists

- looking at the situation from a different perspective

- blaming or criticizing others

- challenging negative thoughts

- thinking positively

- vigorously defending our position

- using positive affirmations

- telling ourselves inspirational quotes like "This too shall pass" or "What does not hurt me makes me stronger"

- trivializing the issue, pretending it's not important, or joking about it

- comparing ourselves to others who are worse off

And last but not least, we've all discovered that putting substances into our bodies—whether it is chocolate, ice cream, pizza, sugar, tea, coffee, aspirin, alcohol, tobacco, recreational drugs, herbal remedies, or prescription medication—often gives short-term relief from painful feelings.

But even with all these clever ways to control our feelings, we continue to suffer psychologically. Think of the happiest day of your life: how long did those joyous, happy feelings last before some anxiety, frustration, disappointment, or irritation showed up? Not long, right? And that's on the happiest day of your life! So when life hits hard, most of these emotion control strategies fail miserably.

To live a full human life, however, is to experience the full range of human emotions—not just the ones that "feel good." Our feelings change like the weather—sometimes pleasant, sometimes extremely uncomfortable. And what would happen if we believed we should have good weather every day? If this was our attitude, how much would we struggle with reality? How much would our life shrink if we told ourselves, *I can't do what really matters to me, or be the person I want to be, unless the weather is good*?

Talking about the weather this way seems ridiculous. We know we can't control the weather, so we don't even try to. We adapt what we do and wear to the weather conditions. But with emotions, most of us do the opposite—we try really hard to control them! This is quite natural. Because we want to feel good, not bad, we try to push our unwanted feelings away with quick fixes such as those mentioned above. And, of course, most of those things reduce pain quite well at times—but for how long? A few minutes? Perhaps a few hours if we're lucky?

As we journey through life, we all experience intense and uncomfortable emotions that we can't simply turn off with the flick of a switch. And you've undoubtedly discovered that the strategies we use to control our emotions often ultimately impair our quality of life in the long run, especially with drugs, alcohol, tobacco, chocolate, and gambling. But if you look closely, with an open mind, you'll find that any emotion control strategy when used *excessively* or *rigidly* can cause problems.

Even something as healthy as exercise will become problematic if we use it *excessively* or *rigidly* to try to control our feelings. For example, some people suffering from anorexia exercise vigorously every day. In the short run, this helps them to control their feelings of anxiety by pushing away all those fears about getting fat, but in the long run, it keeps their bodies in a state of extremely unhealthy thinness. This is obviously very different from exercising *flexibly* in order to look after your health and well-being *wisely*.

Often, the disappointments and setbacks we experience when we attempt to control our emotions just push us to try even harder, to find even cleverer ways to control how we feel. We keep hoping that one day we'll find the ultimate strategy, one that will give us excellent control of our feelings. But sooner or later, we realize this is a lost cause. To emphasize this point, whenever I give workshops or lectures, I ask all the parents in the room to raise their hands. Usually, this is about three-quarters of the audience. I say, "Having a child enriches your life enormously and gives you some of the most wonderful feelings you will ever have—unimaginable love, joy, and tenderness. But are those the only feelings they give you?"

Everyone shakes their head and says, "Nooooo!"

"What other feelings do children give you?" I ask.

There is a cacophony of responses: fear, anger, exhaustion, worry, guilt, sadness, pain, frustration, rejection, boredom, and rage, among others.

And there you have it: the things that make life rich and meaningful give rise to a wide range of feelings, both pleasant *and* painful. (This, of course, holds true for every loving relationship, not just those with our children.)

Unfortunately, it may take us a long time to come to this realization. It may take us a hundred self-help books, or twenty years of therapy, or five different types of prescription medication, or a dozen self-empowerment courses, or decades of silent struggle, or a lifetime of seeking advice from various "experts" before we truly recognize the simple truth: when it comes to painful emotions, we have not been well educated by our society. We have learned only two ways of responding: control or be controlled. And if these are our only two options, we will always struggle.

Sometimes I have clients who react quite negatively to these ideas; they cling to the idea that recovering from their loss means no more painful thoughts and feelings. *If only!* As we recover from our losses and heal our wounds, those difficult thoughts, feelings, and memories don't disappear. Instead, we find a new way of responding to them. We learn how to handle them differently, how to lessen their impact so that when they arise, they can't hold us back from engaging in life. We learn how to access a center of stillness in the midst of our pain, how to create a space within ourselves through which our feelings can freely flow—without pushing us around or bringing us down. I call this "dropping the struggle."

Learning to Drop the Struggle

When we only have two options for responding to difficult thoughts and feelings—control or be controlled—life becomes exhausting, because we invest so much time and energy in this futile struggle with our inner world. But there's a third way of responding to these difficult inner experiences; and it's so radically different to the other two ways, it often takes a while to understand it. So, to get a sense of what it involves, I invite you to do a little experiment.

A Simple Three-Step Experiment

There are three steps to this experiment, and you will get much more out of it if you actually *do* it rather than simply reading about it. This experiment is very important, because it paves the way for the skills we're going to learn in the next chapter—and it requires you to actually pick up your physical copy of this book, or the device you are reading it on.

Step 1: Imagine that in front of you is everything that's important; both the pleasant things—like the people, movies, music, food, books, and activities you love—and the unpleasant things—like all the challenges and problems you have to deal with. And hold this book firmly in your hands and imagine that it contains all the thoughts, feelings, emotions, sensations, urges, and memories that you find most difficult. (Take a few moments to name them.)

Step 2: *(Please don't do this step if you have neck, shoulder, or upper arm problems; instead, just vividly imagine what it would be like to do it.)* When you reach the end of this paragraph, take this book in both hands and grip it tightly around the edges. Now push your arms out as far as you possibly can (without dislocating your shoulders!), keeping your elbows straight and holding the book at arm's length. Hold it like that—pushing it away as hard as you can—for about 1 minute and notice what the experience is like.

Did you find that uncomfortable or tiring? Imagine doing this all day long. How exhausting would it be? And imagine watching your favorite movie or TV show, having a conversation or eating a meal, or making love at the same time as doing this exercise. How much would it distract you or interfere with your enjoyment? This is what controlling our emotions is like: we exert a huge amount of energy into pushing them away. This is not only draining and distracting, but it also pulls us out of the here-and-now and into an internal struggle. When we are trying hard to control our emotions, it's very difficult to be present and respond effectively to life's challenges. Now let's try something different.

Step 3: When you reach the end of this paragraph, again push the book away from you (still imagining it's full of your most difficult thoughts and feelings). Push it as hard as you can, for about 30 to 60 seconds. Then stop pushing, place the book gently on your lap, and let it sit there. Notice the difference this makes. Now, as you let the book sit there, stretch your arms, take a breath, and with a sense of genuine curiosity, scan your surroundings, and notice what you can see and hear around you.

Did you notice how letting the book sit on your lap was so much easier than keeping it at arm's length? Did you notice that when you made space for it, when you stopped struggling with it and pushing it away, you could be fully present with the world around you?

Dropping the struggle, as I called it above, is a radically different way of responding to painful inner experiences. It involves opening up and making room for our thoughts, feelings, and memories. We let them come, stay, and go in their own good time. We're not letting them push us around or sweep us away, nor are we investing our energy in fighting with or running from them.

When I took Shanti through this exercise, she said, "Yes, but this is just a book. I can't do that with real feelings." And she was right. It's easy to rest a book in your lap but a whole lot harder to do something similar with actual thoughts and feelings. But we *can* learn how to do that, as you'll see in the next chapter.

5   When Storms Arise

With great loss comes great pain. Often there is sadness and sorrow, and guilt or regret, especially if we contributed to what happened—or believe that we did. Also, we may experience a lot of anger and fear, because all major losses pose a threat to us. They may threaten our way of life, our security, our physical or mental health, our well-being, our loved ones, or other things we hold dear. As we discussed in chapter 1, when we encounter a significant threat, we immediately go into fight-or-flight mode. But if fight or flight seems futile, the freeze response kicks in. In humans, the fight response fosters anger, irritation, resentment, or rage, while the flight response fosters fear, anxiety, insecurity, or panic. In contrast, the freeze response gives rise to numbness, lethargy, apathy, and fatigue.

Then, on top of that, our minds pour fuel on the fire. They generate anxious, angry, judgmental, or hopeless thoughts, and often dredge up painful memories too. We get hooked by these thoughts and worry about the future, dwell on the past, blame ourselves or others, or obsess about things that are out of our control.

These are normal responses to challenging, uncertain, and unstable situations, so we expect them to happen repeatedly after a major loss. We can think of these reactions as "emotional storms": difficult thoughts blow wildly around inside our head, while intense feelings and emotions whip through our body. And when an emotional storm sweeps us away, it also takes away our ability to effectively deal with the difficult challenges we face.

So how do we handle emotional storms? Well, in real life, when a storm blows into a seaside town, all the boats in the harbor drop anchor. Why?

Because if they don't, they'll be damaged or swept out to sea. But even when a boat drops anchor, the storm doesn't magically go away. Anchors can't control the weather, but they can hold the boat steady until the storm passes. So we're going to do something very similar—and learn how to "drop anchor" when emotional storms rage inside us.

The ACE Formula: Acknowledge, Connect, Engage

Anchor-dropping exercises can be as short as ten seconds or as long as ten minutes, and you can do them anytime, anyplace. There are literally hundreds of ways to drop anchor (and you can easily invent your own), but they use the simple "ACE" formula:

A: **acknowledge** your thoughts and feelings

C: **connect** with your body

E: **engage** in what you're doing

So let's try the ACE formula right now. You can do this exercise no matter how you feel—happy or sad, anxious or angry, neutral or numb.

The ACE Formula in Practice

A: Acknowledge Your Thoughts and Feelings

Silently and kindly acknowledge whatever is "showing up" inside you: thoughts, feelings, emotions, memories, sensation, urges. With the openness and curiosity of a child, notice what's going on in your inner world.

Quickly scan your body for feelings and sensations, and note what kind of thoughts are passing through your head. Often it's helpful to describe this with phrases like "I'm noticing" or "I'm having" (as we discussed in chapter 3). For example, you might say to yourself, *I'm noticing anxiety, I'm having a feeling of sadness, I'm noticing numbness, I'm having scary thoughts, I'm noticing my mind obsessing,* or *I'm having thoughts about being a bad person.*

Acknowledge your thoughts and feelings without judging, fighting, or trying to get rid of them. You're simply acknowledging that—right now, in this moment—they are here.

C: Connect with Your Body

While continuing to acknowledge your thoughts and feelings, connect with your physical body. Try some or all of the following, or find your own way of doing this:

- Slowly push your feet into the floor.

- Slowly straighten your back and your spine.

- Slowly press your fingertips together.

- Slowly stretch your arms or your neck or shrug your shoulders.

If chronic illness or an injury limits what you can do with your physical body, adapt this exercise accordingly. Because of her fibromyalgia and the intense pain in her upper body, Rada avoided most of the movements above, though she could push her feet into the floor. Together we came up with these alternatives:

- Slowly and gently, breathe in and out.

- Slowly and gently, adjust your position in the chair to one that's more comfortable.

- Slowly and gently, move your eyes from side to side.

- Slowly and gently, raise your eyebrows, then lower them.

Be creative; anything that helps you connect with your body will suffice. As you do this, you're not trying to escape, avoid, or distract yourself from what's happening in your inner world. Nor are you trying to get rid of difficult thoughts and feelings. (Remember: anchors don't make storms go away.) The aim is to remain aware of your thoughts and feelings, to acknowledge their presence, and at the same time, connect with your body and actively move it. Why? So you can gain more control over your physical actions—over what you do with your arms, hands, legs, feet, face, and mouth. Trying to control your thoughts and feelings often fails or creates new problems. But taking control of your physical actions will enable you to act effectively as the emotional storm continues to rage.

E: Engage in What You're Doing

Now as you acknowledge your thoughts and feelings, and connect with your body, also get a sense of where you are and refocus your attention on the activity you are doing. Try some or all of the following suggestions, or find your own methods:

- Look around the room and notice five things you can see.

- Notice three or four things you can hear.

- Notice what you can smell or taste, or sense inside your nose or mouth.

- Notice what you are doing.

- End the exercise by giving your full attention to the activity you're doing.

The idea is to run through this ACE cycle slowly three or four times and turn it into a two- to three-minute exercise. To help you with this, I've created free audio recordings of "dropping anchor" exercises (one to eleven minutes long). You can download them from links in my free e-book, *When Life Hits Hard: Extra Bits*, which you'll find on the Free Resources page of www.the happinesstrap.com.

Anchors Don't Control Storms

Sometimes when I take people through this exercise, they complain, "It's not working!" So I ask, "What do you mean?" They usually reply with something like, "I don't feel any better. It's not making these feelings go away." So I explain that just as anchors don't control storms, the ACE formula isn't a way to control your feelings.

The aims of dropping anchor are

- to gain more control of our physical actions so we can act more effectively when difficult thoughts and feelings show up,

- to reduce the impact and influence of our thoughts and feelings: when we're consciously aware of our thoughts and feelings, they lose their control over us, but when we're on autopilot, they jerk us around like a puppet on a string,

- to interrupt worrying, rumination, obsessing, or any other way we get lost inside our heads,

- to interrupt problematic behaviors, such as fighting and arguing with loved ones, withdrawing and hiding away from them, or inappropriately using drugs and alcohol, and

- to help us refocus and engage in the activity we are doing when our thoughts and feelings keep pulling us out of it.

We'll explore other benefits of this practice later, but I'd like to clarify one important thing: *you're not trying to distract yourself* from your difficult thoughts and feelings.

Remember, A is for acknowledge. Acknowledging the thoughts, feelings, emotions, sensations, urges, and memories we're experiencing is the opposite of distraction. If we try to distract ourselves from these inner experiences—try to get away from them, ignore them, pretend that they aren't there—we're right back in the "control or be controlled" struggle we discussed in chapter 4. Distraction's not wrong or bad, but you already know how to do it, and you know it only gives short-term relief. Our aim here is to do something radically different: to step out of that struggle, to let our thoughts and feelings be as they are, to let them come and go in their own good time. Think again of that boat dropping anchor in the harbor—it's not trying to get rid of the storm or distract itself from it. Dropping anchor holds the boat steady while the storm comes and goes in its own good time.

So, if you are in intense emotional pain—for example, if the person you love is dying, or you're flooded with panic or struggling with crushing loneliness—it's highly unlikely that your pain will disappear as you drop anchor. But you can expect that it will lose some of its impact; you'll drain away its power so it can't jerk you around as much. And if you practice for several minutes, you'll often start to experience a sense of calmness, even as your inner storm continues.

However, if you're just feeling a little bit sad or anxious, then as you drop anchor, the pain will often lessen or even disappear. You can enjoy that, of course, when it happens—but keep in mind that's a bonus, not the main aim. If you start using these techniques to try to avoid, escape, get rid of, or distract yourself from painful thoughts and feelings, you'll soon be frustrated and complain that it's not working.

The first time I took Shanti through this exercise, we spent a good five minutes on it, cycling several times through ACE. Her transformation was profound. Her posture changed from hunched over to upright; her voice became stronger and more lively; her facial expression changed from despairing to peaceful; instead of staring at the floor, she looked right at me. I said to her, "You know those moments where the clouds part, and the sunlight comes shining through? That's what this is like for me. Five minutes ago, you were so lost in all those thick black clouds of thoughts and feelings, it was like you'd disappeared from the room, but now, you're back." A warm smile played across her face. Shanti's thoughts and feelings hadn't disappeared (anchors don't make storms go away), but their impact lessened, and now she could fully engage in our session.

Back to the Present

One aim of the anchor-dropping exercise is to strengthen your ability to focus on and engage in what you're doing. Many of us find this challenging at the best of times, but it's exceptionally hard to do after big losses. It's hard to be fully present and attentive, and we often operate on autopilot, doing things poorly because we can't focus. We're even unable to engage fully in activities we once loved. Even when things go well, it's often hard to focus, engage, and be present. But when life hits hard, disengagement and distractibility rise to whole new levels. Again, our fight, flight, or freeze responses contribute to this, so let's take another look at them.

Hunting, as our ancient ancestors did, was a dangerous activity. The further they ventured away from their safe, familiar home territory, the greater the threat. So, if you're out late at night on a hunting mission, you don't stare peacefully into the campfire. Instead, you keep watch for wolves, bears, and rival clans. Fight-or-flight mode encourages this; it predisposes you to keep shifting your attention, which therefore makes it hard to focus or concentrate. What about freeze mode? Well, here your nervous system wants you to lie still and be quiet until the threat has gone, so it helps you to zone out, drift off, and take your attention away from what's going on. During the worst parts of your experience, this helps you escape the horror to some extent, but in the weeks or months that follow, the same response keeps activating, which again makes it hard to engage in or focus on what you're doing. So I hope you'll transfer the basic principles of dropping anchor to everyday life: wherever you are, whatever you're doing, see if you can catch yourself drifting off or zoning out, gently acknowledge it, and then refocus on the activity at hand.

One way our minds pull us out of the present is by dragging us back into the past. One of my clients, Ali, was an Iraqi refugee. He had been horribly tortured under Saddam Hussein's regime. He had dared to publicly criticize the government, so they threw him into prison for several months. During that time, his jailers did the most horrific things to his body. Two years later, as he sat in my office, Ali kept having flashbacks to those events. A *flashback* is a memory that is so vivid and incredibly real that it's as if it is actually happening here and now. If you've never had one, you can scarcely imagine how terrifying it can be.

Whenever Ali tried to talk to me about his time in prison, a flashback would hijack him: his body became rigid, his eyes glazed over, and his face paled. Dragged back into the past, he would relive the torture as if it were happening again. So my first task, before addressing any of his other serious problems, was to teach him how to get himself back to the present.

I asked him to practice dropping anchor at least twenty to thirty times a day. That may seem like a lot, but he was suffering from post-traumatic stress disorder (PTSD), and I knew those flashbacks would repeatedly and unexpectedly hijack him, carrying him off to the past to relive his nightmares. So I wanted him to become an expert at returning to the here and now. And I strongly encourage you to do the same.

After any significant loss, painful memories—about the events that happened, what lead up to them, or what life was like before—can show up repeatedly. When we are grieving, even the most beautiful memories can trigger great pain as we remember all those good times when we were with the person who is no longer there, or doing the job we loved, or doing all those activities we could enjoy before injury or illness made them impossible; all sorts of painful emotions show up. Later in the book, we'll look at ways to work with and handle these memories, but, for now, the aim is simply to drop anchor.

So when a painful memory shows up, begin with A: acknowledge your thoughts and feelings. Say to yourself, *I'm noticing a memory, Here's a painful memory,* or *I'm having a memory.* If possible, specifically label the memory— for example, *Here's a memory of my mother, I'm having a memory of the funeral,* or *I'm noticing a memory of the car crash.* Acknowledge the memory and all the painful feelings that go with it, and then connect with your body and engage in what you're doing.

Antonio found this practice very helpful. He had deeply distressing memories of finding baby Sophia in her crib—unmoving, silent, and blue. Whenever they resurfaced, he'd drop anchor and say to himself, *Here is a memory of Sophia.* Often, he'd add, *This really hurts. Go easy on yourself.* He wouldn't try to push it away or distract himself; he'd acknowledge it and allow it to be there—and at the same time, he'd connect with his body through stretching, and then engage with the world. Over time, this practice made a big difference; the memories still hurt when they resurfaced, but they lost a lot of their impact.

Anytime, Anyplace

We can do an anchor-dropping exercise anytime and anyplace, and it instantly brings us back into the present. We can then engage in life and focus on the task at hand. We don't want to wait until emotional storms begin to blow; practice these exercises throughout the day. We can practice whenever we drift off into our thoughts and feelings, at stoplights, during commercial breaks on the TV, waiting in a line, at our desk before starting work, during our lunch break, or first thing when we get out of bed. We can practice at times when our emotional weather is mild—when we're just a bit grumpy, down, worried. We can practice when we're bored or impatient— instead of turning to our smartphones for distraction. We can practice with any inner experience—thoughts, images, memories, emotions, feelings, sensations, urges, impulses—in any combination.

As with any exercise in this book, you can modify dropping anchor. For instance, when it comes to C—connect with your body—you might choose to stand up and stretch, holding that stretch and feeling your muscles lengthen. You could push your palms and fingers against each other and feel the muscles contract in your neck, arms, and shoulders. You could press your hands down on the arms of your chair or firmly massage the back of your neck and scalp. You could breathe in and out, slowly and gently, or ever so slowly adjust your position in your chair, and notice what your body does to enable that. You could slowly look around the room and notice how you're using your neck, head, and eyes, or, if you know how to do them and you're somewhere private, you could do a move from yoga, tai chi, or Pilates. You could wiggle your toes, tap your feet, shrug your shoulders, twiddle your thumbs, cup your hands, clench your buttocks, give yourself a gentle hug, slide your hands over your knees…or hundreds of other possibilities.

Once you've connected with your body, you move on to E—engage in what you're doing. You notice what you can see, hear, touch, taste, or smell; notice where you are and what you're doing, and refocus on the task at hand.

I recommend you drop anchor

- whenever an emotional storm blows up;

- when you want to disrupt worrying, obsessing, ruminating—
  or any other thinking process that pulls you out of your life;

- when it's hard to focus on or engage in what you're doing—
  when you keep zoning out, drifting off, or going into autopilot;

- when you're in fight-or-flight mode, gripped by anger or fear
  and need to calm down and get control of your actions so you
  can act calmly even though you don't feel it; and

- when you're in freeze mode (shutting down, flopping, slumping, zoning out, disengaging, or, in extreme cases, literally "freezing up") to help you wake up, become energized, take back control of your actions, and help you to engage in what you're doing.

Dropping anchor is an act of self-kindness: a caring and supportive way of responding to your suffering. So, if you've been finding kind self-talk helpful, it's good to actively bring it into this exercise. For example, as you acknowledge your pain, you could say to yourself, *This really hurts. Hold yourself kindly*, or better still, use a phrase of your own.

With so many different options for dropping anchor, you can tailor it to suit your own needs. As long as you're using the ACE formula, you're doing the exercise. You can do it as quickly or as slowly as you like, as often as you want, whatever you're feeling. And if you practice this regularly, it will pay big dividends in terms of health and well-being. It may take a while, though, so please persist and be patient. Remember these words from the great Scottish author, Robert Louis Stevenson: "Don't judge each day by the harvest you reap, but by the seeds that you plant."

6 Psychological Smog

Can you hear it? That voice inside your head? The one that virtually never shuts up? There's a popular misconception that folks who "hear voices" are abnormal, but we all have at least one voice inside our head, and most of us have quite a few! For example, most of us occasionally have inner mental debates between the "voice of reason and logic" and the "voice of doom and gloom," or the "voice of revenge'" and the "voice of forgiveness." And we're all familiar with that self-judgmental voice that's often called the "inner critic." (I once asked a client, "Have you heard of the 'inner critic'?" "Yes," she said, "I've got an inner committee!")

Obviously, the ability to think is incredibly valuable, and it adds enormously to our quality of life. Without the ability to think, we could neither create nor appreciate books, movies, music, or art; nor could we enjoy blissful daydreams, plan for the future, or share our feelings with loved ones. However, many of our thoughts aren't particularly useful. Suppose I plug into your mind, record all your thoughts today, and transcribe them onto paper. Then I ask you to read the transcript and highlight any thoughts that had been *truly helpful* for you in responding effectively to your loss. What percentage of the thoughts would you highlight?

For most of us, the percentage would be small. It's almost as if the mind has a mind of its own; it talks all day long about whatever it pleases, whether this helps us or not. It seems particularly fond of dwelling on pain from the past, worrying about the future, or obsessing about problems in the present. And yet, even though what it has to say is often unhelpful, somehow it almost always manages to absorb us in its stories.

Now, let me clarify what I mean by "stories" because sometimes people take offense at the word: a *story* is a sequence of words or pictures that conveys information. I could say "thoughts" or "cognitions," but calling them "stories" helps us handle them more effectively. You see, our mind tells us stories all day long. If they are "true stories," we call them "facts," but facts make up only a tiny percentage of our thoughts. Our thoughts include all sorts of ideas, opinions, judgments, theories, goals, assumptions, day-dreams, fantasies, predictions, and beliefs that can hardly be called facts. So the word "story" doesn't imply that the thoughts are false, inaccurate, or invalid— it's simply a way of describing what thoughts are: words or pictures that convey information. (If you don't like the term "story," just replace it with "cognition" or "thought.")

Now consider this: how often does your mind keep you awake at night or consume huge chunks of your day with stories that induce guilt, fear, anger, anxiety, sadness, disappointment, or despair? How often does it pull you into stories of blame, resentment, worry, or regret? How often does it get you stressed out, wound up, angry, or anxious, which makes your situation even harder?

If you answered, "Very often," then you have a normal human mind, because that's what normal human minds naturally do. Eastern philoso-phers have known this for thousands of years, but, in the West, we bought into the idea that when the mind operates this way it is "abnormal." Unfortunately, this sets us up to struggle with our minds (which is futile) or to judge ourselves harshly for the way we think (also futile).

Why Our Minds Do What They Do

Ironically, this wonderful instrument we call "the human mind," which is so creative, innovative, and immensely useful to us, came with a built-in ten-dency to judge, compare, and criticize as well as to find fault, focus on defi-ciencies, and see problems everywhere it looks.

Why does the mind work this way? Let's consider it in terms of our ancient ancestors. Many eons ago, the men and women who lived longest were those who could clearly see the current problems (e.g., dangerous animals, brutal weather, and vicious rivals), those who could best anticipate future problems (e.g., those animals, weather, and rivals again), and those who could solve these problems effectively. So if one of our ancient ancestors wandered around blissfully, thinking that everything was good, seeing no problems, and anticipating no problems, then he or she wouldn't have survived long enough to have children—the dangerous animals, brutal weather, or vicious rivals would have killed them first.

Thus, over countless generations our minds have become super-duper problem-solving machines that see problems everywhere: things that are *not good enough* the way they are. The great irony is that our minds aren't trying to make life hard for us—they're actually trying very hard to *help* us: either to help us get something we want, or to protect us from something we don't want. Let's look at some examples.

Worrying and predicting the worst. Your mind is preparing you to get you ready for action. It's saying, "Look out! Bad things are likely to happen. You might get hurt. You might suffer. Get ready. Prepare yourself. Protect yourself."

Ruminating and dwelling on the past. Here your mind helps you learn from past events. It's saying, "Bad stuff happened. If you don't learn from this, it might happen again. So figure this out: Why did it happen? What could you have done differently? Learn from this so you'll know what to do if something similar ever happens again."

Self-criticism, self-blame, self-judgment. Your mind wants to protect you from failure, rejection, disappointment, broken relationships, health problems, or a bazillion other adverse outcomes. It gives you a hard time over things you've done or keep doing, because it wants you to stop; it predicts that if you keep doing these things, something bad will happen. It's trying to help you do things better so you get better outcomes. Same deal when it judges you as "weak," "defective," "worthless," "selfish," "broken," "unlovable," and so on. It's saying you need to change what you're doing, because if you continue this way, bad stuff will happen: rejection, failure, and so on.

Reason giving. Your mind comes up with all sorts of reasons why you can't change, shouldn't change, or shouldn't even have to change—change is too hard, too painful, too scary; you don't have what it takes; or it's hopeless because things can't possibly improve. It's protecting you from getting hurt. It knows that if you step out of your comfort zone and act to improve things, you may fail, and that will be painful. So again, it's trying to save you from painful outcomes and adverse events.

Hopelessness, pointlessness, meaninglessness. In another attempt to save you from pain, your mind says there's *no point trying* to improve things, because life itself is meaningless; just give up, stop caring about anything, treat life as pointless. If you can truly manage not to care about anything, you'll be saved from the pain of rejection, loss, and failure that comes when you *really do* care—as well as all the fear and anxiety that comes when you step out of your comfort zone, all the frustration and disappointment when you don't get what you want. The basic message: "Don't even try, because you'll get hurt even more."

Suicidality. Once again, your mind tries to save you from pain. Life seems unbearable, so your mind figures if you kill yourself, that will stop your suffering. (Note: Suicidal thoughts are very common after major losses. However, this book isn't a treatment for suicidality, so if you are suicidal, please immediately seek professional advice.)

Blaming, revenge, resentment. In an effort to save you from injustice, unfairness, and bad treatment by others, your mind points out what those people have done wrong or considers how to punish them. It aims to help you learn from these past events so you're better prepared to handle future ones.

Self-doubt, insecurity. Many of us experience significant self-doubt, insecurity, or indecision after a big loss: We ask ourselves: *Am I handling this right? Am I making the right decisions, doing the right things—or am I screwing it up? Can I handle this? Can I do this?* Again, your mind tries to protect you: watch out, be careful, this is new territory, there are new game rules, you could get hurt. This may raise questions like *Who am I? Who am I without my job? Who am I without my partner...my parents...my child? Who am I without my health?* Here your mind wants you to think deeply about what sort of person you want to be, what values you want to live by, what you want to stand for in the face of your loss. (We'll be exploring these questions in depth in part 2, Rebuild.)

Vulnerability. After a major loss, our sense of vulnerability may be heightened, and we don't feel as strong or invincible as we used to. We might feel the world is not safe, life is unpredictable, bad things happen to good people, and we can no longer fully trust ourselves, others, or the universe. These thoughts and feelings arise when our minds remind us of a truth we often forget: we *are* vulnerable. Our minds are telling us to look after ourselves, to practice self-care; attend to our emotional, physical, psychological, and spiritual health; and to do the same for our loved ones.

Foreboding, doom, and death anxiety. When a loss involves death, many experience a sense of doom or foreboding, or an increased awareness of the inevitability of our own death. Here your mind reminds you that life is precious and you never know how long you have left, so make the most of it. (We'll look at how to do this in part 3, Revitalize.)

I'm going to stop here, but hopefully you get the point. Whatever unhelpful stuff your mind does, it's basically a misguided attempt to help you, to save you from pain, or help you get more of what you want. Have you ever had an overly helpful friend, one who tries so hard to help you that they become a nuisance? When your mind churns out stories like those above, try to think of it as an overly helpful friend who's trying hard to help—but doing it the wrong way.

Cease the Battle

Many popular psychology approaches encourage you to battle that voice in your head. They tell you to challenge, dispute, or invalidate those "negative" thoughts and replace them with "positive" ones—what a seductive proposition! It appeals to our common sense: stomp on the "bad" thoughts and replace them with "good" ones. But the problem is, if we start a war with our own thoughts, we will never win. Why? Because there's an infinite number of those so-called "negative" thoughts, and no one has ever found a way of eliminating them.

Zen masters, who are like the Olympic athletes of mind training, know this all too well. There's a classic Zen tale about an eager monk who asks his abbot, "How can I find the greatest Zen master in the land?" The abbot replies, "Find the man who claims he has eliminated all negative thoughts. And when you find this man…you know that's not him!"

Yes, we can all learn to think more positively, but that won't stop our minds from generating all sorts of painful, unhelpful stories. Why not? Because learning to think more positively is like learning to speak a new language: if you learn to speak Hungarian, you won't suddenly forget how to speak English.

So if our only way of dealing with those thoughts is to battle with them and replace negative thoughts with positive ones, then we will suffer unnecessarily. Why? Because for most people, this really doesn't work very well in the long run. Usually what happens is the thoughts disappear for a while, but like zombies in a horror movie, they soon return.

A Smoky Haze

We have many ways of talking about this human tendency to get caught up in our thoughts. We might use colorful metaphors like "He's a million miles away," "Her head's in the clouds," "He's lost in thought," or we might talk of worrying, ruminating, rehashing the past, stressing out, obsessing, or being preoccupied.

Basically, this incredibly valuable, uniquely human ability to generate thoughts can leave us wandering around in a smoky haze, lost in our thoughts, and missing out on life. Of course, smoky haze isn't necessarily bad. The smoky haze of incense sticks can be soothing and relaxing. The smoky haze of a bonfire can be exhilarating and fun. But what happens when the smoke gets too thick? You start to cough, your nose runs, and your eyes water. And, if you keep inhaling all that smoke, you will eventually damage your lungs. Similarly, there's a time and place where being absorbed in our thoughts is life-enhancing: daydreaming on a beach, mentally rehearsing an important speech, creating new ideas for a project. But most of us get the balance wrong; we spend way too much time inside our minds, and we wander through our days in a thick cloud of "psychological smog."

And nothing thickens that smog like a major loss. The greater the discrepancy between the life we have now and the life we had before, the more our minds protest. There might be denial (*This can't be happening*), anger (*This shouldn't have happened!*), or despair (*I can't cope, I'll never get over this*). Our minds may agonize over the unfairness of it all, or compare our life to the lives of others and find it wanting, or conjure up all manner of terrible future scenarios. Our minds may go round and round in circles, trying to make sense of it all: *Why me? Why now? How could this happen? Why do bad things happen to good people? What did I do to deserve this?* Our minds may tell us that *Life sucks, This is unbearable, I'm too weak, I'm a bad person, I'm not getting over this fast enough, Life's too hard, It's my fault, They're to blame, You can't trust them,* or thousands of similar judgmental comments.

And as I've said before, these thinking patterns are all very normal—they're just not very helpful. Getting caught in these thoughts will usually increase both our struggle and our pain!

Before we go any further, I'd like to clarify one thing: *our thoughts are not the problem*. Our thoughts do not create psychological smog. It's *the way we respond* to our thoughts that creates the smog. Let's explore this a little further.

What Are Thoughts?

In essence, thoughts are pictures and words in our heads. Don't take my word for this; check it out for yourself. Stop reading, and for one minute, close your eyes and notice your thoughts. Notice where they seem to be located, whether they are moving or still, and whether they are more like pictures, words, or sounds. (Sometimes your mind gets shy when you attempt this; your thoughts disappear and refuse to come out. If this happens, just notice the empty space and silence inside your head and wait patiently. Sooner or later your mind will start up again, even if only to say, *I haven't got any thoughts!*)

What did you notice? If your mind went blank at first, you would have noticed an empty space and silence. But eventually some thoughts showed up, and presumably they were words that you could see, sense, or hear, or pictures you could see, or a combination of both. (If you noticed a sensation or feeling in your body, then that's exactly what it is: a sensation or feeling. Don't confuse those with thoughts.)

When we allow these words and pictures to come and go freely like birds in the sky, they create no problems. But when we hold onto them tightly, *that* is when they turn into smog and pull us out of our life. All the richness of life is lost. We can't taste the sweetness for the smoke. On the other side of that smog, there might be the greatest show on earth, but we wouldn't know it. If you've ever spent time inside this smog, you know how impenetrable it can be; even though we're surrounded by limitless opportunities to enhance and enrich our life, we are completely unable to see them.

Unhooking from Our Thoughts

There are many types of psychological smog, and when we're in the thick of one, we have a hard time navigating our course and dealing with the obstacles we encounter. In ACT, we have a metaphorical name for this state—being *hooked*. When our thoughts "hook us," they dominate us; they reel us in like a fish on a line, and jerk us around like a puppet on a string. When our thoughts hook us, they have enormous power over us. They seem to be commands we must obey, threats we must avoid, obstacles we need to eliminate, or something very important to which we must give our full attention.

In stark contrast, when we "unhook" from our thoughts, they lose their power over us. *Unhooking* means we separate from our thoughts and see them for what they truly are: constructions of words and pictures. When we unhook from our thoughts, they no longer dominate us, we don't have to obey them or give them all our attention, and we don't have to try to get rid of them. Instead, we see their true nature; we recognize that they are nothing more or less than words and pictures; and we allow them to come, stay, and go in their own good time.

Naturally, if our thoughts are *helpful*—if they help us to be kind and compassionate to ourselves, or to behave more like the person we want to be, to make effective plans and take effective action to enrich and enhance our lives in practical ways—then we make good use of them. We don't let them *control* us—push us around, dictate what we do —but we do let them *guide* us.

When we adopt this approach to our thoughts, we are rarely, if ever, concerned as to whether or not they are true. What we're interested in is, are they helpful—will they *help* us adapt to our loss? If we let these thoughts guide us, will we act effectively, behaving like the sort of person we want to be—or will they do the very opposite?

As Rada grappled with all the problems arising from her fibromyalgia, her mind would repeatedly trot out a litany of harsh self-critical thoughts: *Look how pathetic I am. I can't dance, can't cook, can't socialize. I'm useless.* Her previous therapist had tried hard to challenge these thoughts; to look for evidence to disprove them and replace them with more positive thoughts. This hadn't helped at all. I said to her, "Your mind loves to give you a hard time, doesn't it?"

"I deserve it," she said. "Look how pathetic I am."

"And when your mind beats you up that way, does it help you to deal with your condition?"

She paused for a moment, then answered softly, "No."

"Okay, so we're never going to get into a debate about whether your thoughts are true or false, or whether you deserve such harsh judgments. Instead, can we just acknowledge that (a) those thoughts keep showing up, and (b) when you get hooked by them, that makes life harder, not easier."

"Okay."

"Good. So given that state of affairs, how about we work on some unhooking skills? Let's not debate whether these thoughts are true or not; let's just learn how to unhook from them."

Of course, if our thoughts are helpful, we are wise to actively *use* them. (You'll see this clearly in part 2 of the book, where we focus on taking action to rebuild our lives.) But if they're unhelpful, it's best to unhook, to let them come and go, as if they are cars driving past our house.

If you're anywhere near a road right now, listen for the sounds of traffic. Sometimes there's a lot of traffic outside and sometimes there's very little.

But what happens if we try to make the traffic stop? Can we do it? Can we magically wish it away? And what happens if we get angry at the traffic, if we pace up and down, ranting and raving about it? Does this help us live with the traffic? Isn't it easier just to let those cars come and go, and then invest our energy in something more useful?

Suppose a noisy old car drives slowly past your house, engine roaring, exhaust spewing, and loud music booming. You look out of the window and see the car, covered with rust and graffiti, with a group of young guys inside, singing along, whooping it up, shouting obscenities. What's the best thing to do? To run out of the house and yell, "Go away. You have no right to be here!"? To patrol the street all night long to ensure the car doesn't come back? To attempt to keep such cars away in the future, by asking the universe to provide only beautiful cars outside your house? The easiest and simplest approach is to just let that car come and go: acknowledge its presence and allow it to pass through in its own good time. To give you a sense of how to do this, try this experiment.

Another Simple Three-Step Experiment

This experiment is quite similar to the book-pushing exercise in chapter 4, but there are important differences, so please don't skip it.

Step 1: Imagine that in front of you right now is everything that's important in your life. This includes both the pleasant things—like the people you love, and all the movies, music, food, books, activities you enjoy—and the unpleasant things—like the challenges and problems you have to face and deal with. And firmly grasp this book (or reading device) in your hands, and imagine it contains all the thoughts and memories that you find most difficult. (Take a few moments to name them.)

Step 2: When you reach the end of this paragraph, hold this book tightly around the edges, while keeping it open. Gripping the edges tightly, lift the open book up in front of your face, then bring it in so close that it's almost touching your nose—the book should virtually be wrapped around your face, completely obscuring your view of your surroundings. Hold it like that for about 20 seconds and notice what the experience is like.

What did you discover? While you were totally "caught up" in your thoughts and memories, did you feel cut off and disconnected from the important things in your life? Did it seem as if your thoughts dominated everything?

That's what it's like when we're hooked by our thoughts and memories: we get lost in them, consumed by them, or overwhelmed by them. They dominate our experience, making it hard for us to engage in or appreciate the enjoyable and pleasant aspects of life, or to respond effectively to the problems and challenges we face.

Step 3: When you reach the end of this paragraph (again pretending this book is your thoughts and memories), place the book gently on your lap and let it sit there for 20 seconds. And as you let it sit there, stretch your arms, breathe deeply, and with a sense of genuine curiosity, scan your surroundings and notice what you can see and hear around you.

Did you notice how it was much less distracting when the book was sitting on your lap and how it was so much easier to focus on and engage in the world around you? Of course, it's easy to do this with a book, but a whole lot harder with real thoughts. So, in the next chapter, let's do it for real!

7   Notice and Name

Have you ever walked around in *real* smog? When you're in it, you know it: it's hard to breathe, and difficult to see. But when we're lost in *psychological* smog, we usually don't realize it—so we worry, ruminate, or obsess for hours on end.

Thus, the first step in unhooking from our thoughts is simply *to notice* that we're hooked. This is a bit like catching and righting yourself just as you trip or abruptly realizing, midconversation, that you haven't been listening and now you have no idea what the other person is talking about. It's an "Aha!" moment; a gentle jolt, like suddenly waking up from a snooze. I invite you to see, throughout the day, if you can notice when and where your psychological smog arises. Is it in your car, riding your bike, at work, at home, in bed, during dinner, playing with your kids, having a shower, talking to your partner, walking the dog? Try to recall what precipitates the smog: an argument, a rejection, a failure, an unfair act, someone's facial expression, a piece of news (good or bad), a person, a song, the mention of a loved one's name, or something else?

Notice the kinds of smog that trap you: worrying, blaming, self-criticism, hopelessness, obsessing, wishful thinking, dwelling on problems, reliving past horrors, or predicting the worst for the future. This is useful information for the next step.

The Art of Naming

The second step in unhooking is to *name* the thought or thinking process; this gives us some distance from our thoughts. It's like waking from a nightmare. First, you notice that you're awake and in your bedroom. Next, you name the experience: "It was only a dream." As you do this, you wake up further; the dream becomes more distant, the bedroom more present.

The good news is you've already learned how to do this with the kind self-talk in chapter 3 and the "acknowledging" step when you drop anchor. Our aim now is to develop this skill further, to ramp it up, and give it more "oomph." So let's try this with a thought that has a strong negative impact on you—perhaps a harsh self-judgment like *I'm bad, I'm worthless, I'm weak, I'm damaged goods* or a scary thought like *I'm sick, I'll never recover, I can't keep going*. Once you've chosen your thought, you're ready to start this exercise.

Naming Exercise

Step 1: Say the thought to yourself, let it hook you, buy into it as much as you possibly can.

Step 2: As soon as you sense that you're hooked, notice the thought and name it. Below are five naming techniques; I invite you to try them all to see which works best:

- I'm having the thought that…

- I'm noticing the thought that…

- Here's my mind telling me that…

- I notice my mind telling me that…

- I notice I'm having the thought that…

Please try this now, before reading on. For example, if your mind tells you that you're useless, say to yourself, *I'm useless.* Let it hook you and reel you in. Once you're hooked, say to yourself, *I'm having the thought that "I'm useless."* Try this with two or more thoughts, and use two or three different naming techniques. Notice what happens.

I hope that was useful. When we notice and name a thought, we usually unhook from it, at least a little. That doesn't necessarily mean the thought disappears; sometimes it will, sometimes it won't. Nor does it mean we'll feel better; sometimes we will, sometimes we won't. This technique doesn't rid us of unwanted thoughts or control our feelings—so if we use it that way, we'll soon be disappointed or frustrated. Instead, this is a way to lessen the power of a thought so it no longer dominates us, pulls us into self-defeating behaviors, or distracts us so we can't focus on or engage in what we're doing.

If this doesn't happen right away, the next step is to drop anchor. We run through the ACE formula, and we bring naming into the "acknowledge" component. As we acknowledge the thoughts that are present, we say to ourselves, *I'm noticing thoughts about being hopeless—and feelings of sadness and despair.* We then connect with our body and engage in what we're doing, then repeat as needed.

Naming the Pattern

Often so many thoughts whir through our head that it's not practical to name each one. In such cases, it's better to name the thinking pattern itself. For instance, when we notice thoughts about things that might go wrong, we could name it "worrying" or "predicting the worst." If we're dwelling on grievances and grudges, we might name that "blaming" or "resentment." If we're going over our problems without reaching any useful outcomes, we might call it "stewing" or "ruminating." If we're lost in painful memories, we might call it "pulling me into the past." If we're beating our-selves up, we might call it "judging" or "self-criticism." And if you're not sure what to name it, you can always use the catch-all term "thinking."

Please play with this concept. You may prefer phrases like "Here's my mind judging," "Here's worrying," "I'm noticing blaming," "I'm noticing my mind pulling me into the past," "Here's my mind hooking me," or perhaps simply "Getting hooked." Try to find a term that allows you to quickly name what your mind is doing. Here's how this might play out:

First, you notice that you're hooked.

Then you notice what's hooking you.

Next, you give that thought pattern a name: *Aha! Here's worrying.*

As you name it, notice what it is: a construction of words and pictures.

And then, without trying to avoid or escape these thoughts, notice where you are and what you're doing.

And in that moment, you may notice a sense of lightness, as if the smog has thinned and you now see the world with greater clarity.

If that doesn't happen right away, then run through your anchor-dropping routine:

A: **acknowledge** what's hooking you

C: **connect** with your body

E: **engage** in what you're doing.

This simple exercise is very empowering because it reminds us where our true power lies: not in trying to stop these stories from arising or doing battle with them, but in stepping back, seeing them for what they are, and refocusing our attention where it's needed.

Naming the Story

"Naming the story" is a popular alternative to naming the pattern. Imagine you're writing a book or making a documentary about your current loss, and in some magical way you're going to put all your painful thoughts, feelings, and memories into it. You'll give it a title beginning with the word "the" and ending with the word "story." For example, you might call it The Life's Over Story, The Old and Lonely Story, or The Never-Get-Over-This Story. The title needs to

- summarize the main issue, and

- acknowledge that it's a huge source of pain in your life.

Use a humorous title if you wish, but not a mocking, demeaning, or trivializing one. (If you try this technique and feel belittled, demeaned, or invalidated, then please either change the title or forget this method and stick with naming the pattern.) Once you've created a title, use it to enhance the naming process: any time a thought, feeling, or memory linked to this loss arises, notice it and name it. For instance, *Aha! There it is again: The Life's Over Story.*

A while ago, a middle-aged psychologist—let's call her Naomi—attended one of my workshops. During the midmorning coffee break, Naomi confided that she had a malignant brain tumor. She had tried both conventional medical treatments as well as many alternative ones (meditation, prayer, faith healing, creative visualization, homeopathy, diets and herbal remedies, positive thinking, and self-hypnosis) but, sadly, the tumor was incurable and Naomi didn't have much longer to live. She was attending my workshop to help herself cope with her fear and to make the most of her remaining life. Naomi told me it was difficult to focus in the workshop. She was continually hooked by thoughts of death: she kept thinking of her loved ones and how they would react, "seeing" her MRI scans and that tumor spreading through her brain, and dwelling on the likely progression of her illness—from paralysis to coma, then death.

Clearly, if we're terminally ill, it's often helpful to think about the implications: to consider what we put in our will, what sort of funeral we want, what we wish to say to our loved ones, and what sort of medical care we need to arrange. But if you've gone to a workshop for personal growth, then it's unhelpful to be fused with such thoughts at that time; you won't benefit from the workshop. I listened compassionately to Naomi. After first acknowledging how much pain she was in, empathizing with her fear, and validating how difficult it was for her, we talked about naming the story. (If I had leaped straight into this, she probably would have felt upset or invalidated, as if I were trying to "fix" or "save" her without truly understanding or caring about what she was experiencing.) So Naomi came up with The Scary Death Story.

I asked her to practice naming that story whenever she saw it coming, or whenever she became aware it had hooked her. She did this enthusiastically, and by lunchtime on day two of the workshop, she was pretty unhooked from all those morbid thoughts. The thoughts had not altered in believability—she still considered them all to be true—but she was now able to let them come and go like passing cars and remain engaged in the workshop.

If you want, you can bring in some lightness and humor. For instance, you might playfully say to yourself, *Tut, tut! It's just noooooooooot good enough!* or *I guess The Not Good Enough Show just started* or *Aha! Here it is again. The old I'm Weak Story. I know this one!* (Do be careful if you try this; if you feel belittled, mocked, or trivialized at all, drop the humor or go back to "naming the pattern.")

Thanking Your Mind

Earlier we discussed how the mind is like an overly helpful friend trying hard to help but going about in the wrong way. We explored how ruminating, worrying, self-judging, blaming, hopelessness, and so on is basically your mind trying to save you from getting hurt. Knowing this, it can be helpful to "thank your mind" for its input. For example, after you've noticed and named the thought, pattern, or story, you might say to yourself—again, with a sense of playfulness—*Thanks, mind. I know you're trying to help, but it's okay, I've got this covered. I'll deal with it myself.*

Not everyone finds this technique useful, but most people do. (It's one of my favorites.) Sometimes people say to me, "Why should I thank my mind? It's making my life miserable!" I reply, "It's just a playful way of lessening the impact of those thoughts. It's to help you take them less seriously, to stop fighting with them or trying to push them away." If they're not convinced, I don't try to persuade them; no technique is suitable for everyone. But I *do* encourage you to try this and see how it works for you, because usually it helps us unhook a little bit more; but if it's not helpful, or you don't like the idea of it, use something else.

Neutralizing

Noticing and naming our thoughts is usually enough to break their grip on us. If not, adding anchor dropping or thanking your mind usually does the job. However, sometimes we need to go further and use something I call "neutralizing"—we do something to our thoughts to "neutralize" their power and to help us see them simply as a construction of words and pictures. Neutralization techniques include silently singing your thoughts to popular tunes, saying them to yourself in different voices, drawing them in thought bubbles, visualizing them on a computer screen, imagining them coming from cartoon characters or historical figures, and more. In appendix A, you'll find several neutralizing exercises, so if you need more help with unhooking from your thoughts, please go there and play with the techniques before reading on.

We can't stop our minds from telling us stories, but we can learn to catch them in the act. And we can learn to choose the way we respond: to let the helpful stories guide us and let the unhelpful ones go.

8   Live and Let Be

What's the big deal about breathing? Why do so many spiritual traditions get excited about it? In the Old Testament of the Bible, God formed man from the dust of the ground—and then breathed life into him through the nostrils. In Greek mythology, Prometheus created man out of mud—and then Athena breathed life into him. Our word "spirit" comes from the Latin *spiritus*, "soul" or "breath." Likewise, in Hebrew, the word *ruah* means "breath" or "wind" but also "soul." Similarly, the Greek word *psyche*, the root of "psychology" and "psychiatry," means "soul,", "spirit," or "breath." And contemplative or mystical branches of the world's most popular religions—including Christianity, Islam, Hinduism, Sikhism, Buddhism, and Judaism—include breathing exercises to help one access a higher state of awareness or a direct experience of the divine.

So why this strong connection between breath and spirituality? First is the link between breathing and life. When you breathe, you're alive. Second, breathing exercises are often quite soothing or relaxing. They help us to access a sense of inner peace, to find a safe, calm place. Third, we can use our breath to anchor ourselves in the present. When we're all caught up in our thoughts and feelings, we can focus on our breath to ground ourselves and reconnect with our here-and-now experience.

We're about to explore two exercises that focus on breathing—but first, a few words of caution. Most people benefit from these sorts of exercises, which is why you find forms of them in many self-help books. However, a few people, when they focus on or modify their breathing, have unpleasant reactions such as dizziness, light-headedness, pins and needles, a tight chest, or anxiety. These are very unlikely, but if any of these occur, please do one of the following: (a) if the exercise focuses mainly on the breath (like those in this chapter), simply skip it; (b) if breathing is *not* the main focus, but there are a few instructions such as "breathe into it" or "take a slow breath" (as in some exercises in later chapters), then simply ignore those instructions and do the rest of the exercise.

Now I invite you to do a brief exercise. You may be able to do this while you read, or you may need to read the instructions first, then put the book down to do it.

Take a Breath, Hold, and Let Go

Slowly take a deep breath, and once your lungs are filled with air, hold your breath.

Hold the breath for as long as you possibly can.

Notice how, as you keep the breath trapped inside your body, the pressure steadily builds.

Notice what happens in your chest, neck, and abdomen.

Notice the tension building and the pressure rising. Notice the changing feelings in your head, neck, shoulders, chest, and abdomen. And hold that breath.

Keep holding.

Notice how the sensations grow stronger and more unpleasant, how your body tries ever more forcefully to make you exhale.

Observe those physical sensations as if you are a curious child who has never encountered anything like this before.

And when you can't hold your breath a moment longer, slowly and ever so gently release it.

As you let go, savor the experience. Appreciate the simple pleasure of breathing out. Notice the letting go.

Notice the release of tension.

Notice your lungs deflating and your shoulders dropping. Appreciate the simple pleasure of letting go.

How did you find that experience? Were you able to appreciate it? Did you notice a sense of grounding or centering yourself? Perhaps a sense of calmness or stillness?

How often do we hold on to things, refusing to let go? We hold on to old hurts, grudges, and grievances. We hold on to unhelpful attitudes and prejudices or notions of blame and unfairness. We hold on to self-limiting beliefs, old failures, and painful memories as well as unrealistic expectations of ourselves, the world, or others. We hold on to stories of "right" and "wrong" and "fair" and "unfair" that pull us into fruitless struggles with reality.

Unfortunately, the phrase "let it go" is often misunderstood. It doesn't mean "make it go away" or "get rid of those difficult thoughts and feelings." It means loosen your grip on those thoughts and feelings, instead of holding them so tightly; allow them to come and go in their own good time, without getting caught up in them.

"Let it go" really means "Let it be"—allow it to be as it is. Instead of resisting, fighting, grappling with reality, we acknowledge this is how it is. We stop battling reality, because reality always wins. This doesn't mean we give up on our lives. It means we acknowledge that often when we're ruminating, worrying, obsessing, entangled in our thoughts and feelings, it simply doesn't help. It doesn't change reality. It doesn't help us adapt to life as it is in this moment or do anything effective in response to our problems and challenges.

Imagine if we could catch ourselves whenever we hold on tightly to frustration, criticism, judgment, resentment, or blame, and use our breath to remind us to "let it go." What difference might that make in our relationships, our health, and our vitality?

I now invite you to try another exercise.

Take a Breath, Count to Three

As slowly as possible, take a deep breath in. Then hold it for a count of three. Then slowly, gently exhale.

As you breathe out, let your shoulders drop and feel your shoulder blades sliding down your back.

Notice the sense of release.

Appreciate the simple pleasure of exhaling.

Notice what it's like to let...it...go.

Now do this again.

Slowly breathe in, and hold it for a count of three. Then exhale as slowly and gently as possible.

As you exhale, let your shoulders drop.

Again, appreciate the simple pleasure of exhaling.

And notice what it's like to let...it...go.

I encourage you to try this exercise regularly and see what difference it makes. Try it when you hold on tightly to something—some hurt, resentment, or blame that drains away your vitality. Begin by noticing and naming what has hooked you: *Here's blame* or *I'm noticing anger* or *Here's my mind dwelling on the past.* Then breathe, hold, and exhale. It may be helpful to silently say, *Letting go* or *Let it be.*

Suppose you're stewing over that fight you had with your partner, replaying the unkind comments your boss made, feeling guilty because you lost your temper with the kids, or dwelling on how unfair life is. These forms of "holding on tightly" don't help but merely increase stress and drain your vitality. So, once you notice yourself holding on, simply name what's hooking you, take a deep breath, hold it for three, and then, very slowly… let…it…go.

9 Our Allies Within

Out of the shadows, a deformed hand appears. Two of the fingers are missing their tips; the other two and the thumb are mere stumps. Between those two larger fingers, there's a smoking cigar. Then the smoker's terrifying face—swollen, covered with lumps and sores—emerges from the darkness. He asks, "Do you like cigars?"

You may recognize this scene from the old movie *Papillon*. In this tense moment, the hero falls into a dark trench and finds himself face to face with a leper. As a child, this scene really frightened me. I had no idea what leprosy was, but I knew it was dreadful and I feared I might catch it. Years later, at medical school, I learned how leprosy causes such horrible disfigurations. It's a bacterial infection with many adverse effects on the body—one of the worst is severe nerve damage to the arms and legs. The damaged nerves lose their ability to feel pain. Normally, when you place your hand on a hot metal plate, the pain instantly makes you draw your hand away. Imagine how many injuries you'd sustain, and how much worse they'd be, if you couldn't feel pain. Because lepers can't feel pain, they experience terrible damage to their hands, feet, fingers, and toes—and that brings us the main point of this chapter: pain serves a purpose.

We've talked a lot about pain in this book, which is understandable, given how much loss hurts. But *why* do we have these painful thoughts and feelings? What useful purpose do they serve?

In chapter 6, we discussed this with regard to painful thoughts. We looked at how those painful things that minds do—worrying, ruminating, self-judging—all serve a purpose: our minds are trying to protect us, save us, look out for us. Similarly, in chapter 1, we saw how the nervous system clicks us into fight, flight, or freeze mode to protect us from harm and danger. So now let's explore the three main purposes of our emotions.

Communicate, Motivate, Illuminate

Our emotions are basically messengers that come to us with important information, trying to help us. They have three main purposes: communicate, motivate, illuminate.

Communicate

When others can read our emotions, it allows us to communicate with each other in valuable ways. For example:

- Fear communicates "Watch out; there's danger!" or "I find you threatening."

- Anger communicates "This isn't fair or right," "You're trespassing on my territory," or "I'm defending what's mine."

- Sadness communicates "I've lost something important."

- Guilt communicates "I've done something wrong and I want to put it right."

- Love communicates "I appreciate you," "I want you to stay close."

When we're with people who care about us, people we can trust, these communications are often very valuable. For example, if a good friend sees you're scared or sad, she'll often respond with kindness and support. If she sees you feel guilty for something you did that hurt her, that'll often help to repair the damage done. If she sees you're angry about something she's doing, she might back off and reconsider it. Obviously, we sometimes "send the wrong signals," or others misinterpret them or react negatively; no system works perfectly. But most of the time, as a means of communication, emotions work pretty well.

Motivate

Our emotions also motivate. The words "emotion," "motivate," "motion," and "move" all originate from the Latin word *movere*, which means "to move." Emotions prepare us to move our body in particular ways and to act in ways that are likely to be helpful and life-enhancing. For example:

- Fear motivates us to run away, hide, take evasive action, protect ourselves.

- Anxiety motivates us to prepare ourselves for things that might hurt or harm us.

- Anger motivates us to stand our ground, to fight for what we care about.

- Sadness motivates us to slow down, ease up, take a break, rest up, and recuperate.

- Guilt motivates us to reflect on our behavior and how it's affecting others, and to make amends if we've hurt them.

- Love motivates us to be loving and nurturing, to share and to care.

However, at times emotions show up when they aren't helpful; they hook us and pull us into problematic behaviors. But most often, these emotions *do* work pretty well, provided we don't struggle with them. If we fight with or run from emotions, we create big problems for ourselves. Remember the book-pushing exercise in chapter 4? Strongly pushing it away ate up your energy, distracted you, and made it hard to act effectively. But if we drop the struggle with our emotions, make room for them, let them flow through us—as you'll learn to do in chapter 10—we'll find we can often make use of them in life-enhancing ways.

Illuminate

Finally, our emotions illuminate what's important to us. They alert us that something is happening that matters, something we need to attend to. They "shine a light" on our deepest needs and wants. For example:

- Fear illuminates the importance of safety and protection.

- Anger illuminates the importance of defending our territory, protecting a boundary, or standing up and fighting for what is ours.

- Sadness illuminates the importance of rest and recuperation after a loss.

- Guilt illuminates the importance of how we treat others and the need to repair social bonds.

- Love illuminates the importance of connection, intimacy, bonding, caring, and sharing.

Our emotions contain much wisdom, but we can't access this wisdom when we fight with or distract ourselves from them, but when we open up and make room for them (see chapter 10), it's a different story. Later, we'll learn how to extract this wisdom from our thoughts and feelings, and use it to help us rebuild our lives. Hopefully, by now, you're starting to see that our emotions are our allies, not our enemies.

Missing Out

In *Dubliners,* James Joyce writes, "Mr. Duffy lived a short distance from his body." I love this quote. To be honest, I haven't read *Dubliners,* so I've no idea why Mr. Duffy lived a short distance from his body, but I can tell you he's not the only one. At times, most of us are disconnected from our bodies, especially when they're full of painful feelings. This makes sense. We'd stay out of the water, if we knew a great white shark lurked there. Similarly, we stay out of our bodies if we know we'll encounter painful feelings there.

At times, the autonomic nervous system makes this decision for us: it "cuts off" our emotions, leaving us numb. More commonly, we numb ourselves: with medication, drugs, or alcohol. And most commonly of all, we escape from our bodies through distraction. The word "distraction" comes from two Latin words: *dis,* which means "apart," and *trahere,* which means "to draw." So when we distract ourselves, we "draw apart" from something unpleasant or unwanted. When we distract ourselves from painful feelings, we "draw apart" from the body that houses them.

The more we lose touch with our bodies, the more problems this causes. Perhaps the most common is the awful sense of lifelessness it fosters, which people describe as being numb, empty, hollow, dead inside, an empty husk, a shell, a zombie, a walking corpse, feeling nothing, half alive, barely alive, or lifeless. These words describe a state that is the very opposite of "vitality."

The word "vitality" comes from the Latin *vita,* meaning "life." Vitality refers to the life force within us: our energy, drive, and passion; our appreciation of life; our ability to feel fully alive and participate fully in the world. Our bodies keep us alive, and our feelings remind us we're alive; so it's hardly surprising that when we disconnect from them, we lose our vitality.

But the problems don't stop there. A wealth of scientific research shows that when we cut ourselves off from our bodies, we lose that emotional wisdom we discussed above, which in turn leads us to suffer in many ways. For example:

- We have less control over our impulses and urges, which makes us more prone to behaviors such as aggression, drug and alcohol abuse, or overeating.

- We lack self-awareness and our judgment is impaired, often leading to "bad decisions," which we later regret.

- We have difficulty reading the emotions of others, which, combined with lack of self-awareness, gives rise to conflict and tension in relationships.

- We have difficulty being intimate with others, which leads to disconnection and loneliness.

Many people are surprised about these side effects of emotional disconnection, so I'd like to briefly explain why they happen.

The Side Effects of Emotional Disconnection

Remember when you were a kid and your teacher left the classroom? What happened? All hell broke loose, right? Well, it's the same thing with our emotions. Our awareness is like the teacher, and our emotions are like the kids. If we're not aware of our feelings, they act up, create havoc, and riot. The less aware we are of our feelings, the more they control our actions; they jerk us around and pull us into problematic behavior. When the teacher returns to the classroom, the kids immediately settle down. Same deal when we bring awareness to our feelings; they lose their impact and their ability to jerk us around.

Of course, when the teacher's gone, she has no idea what the kids are up to. It's much the same for us when we disconnect from our feelings; we call this "a lack of self-awareness." Did anyone ever say to you, "You seem in a bad mood," ""Why are you so grumpy?" or "You seem down, are you okay?" If so, did it surprise you? Did you respond, "I'm not" or "No, I'm fine!" Did you ever raise your voice or snap at someone without knowing why? Or overeat, drink too much, or cry a lot for "no obvious reason"? Or make decisions that you later judged as "stupid" and wondered, *Why did I do that?* These common scenarios all point to a lack of emotional awareness.

As we interact with others, our body continuously generates feelings based on what's happening. These feelings are a gold mine of information, if we can access them. To briefly switch metaphors, have you ever watched a movie without the sound on? (If you haven't, please try it for a minute.) How diminished is the experience? The images are great, but without the music, the dialogue, the sound effects, we lose so much. We generally know what's happening, but it's less satisfying and we can easily misread what's going on. This is what it's like when we interact with others while cut off from our own emotions. Our relationships suffer because we misread people—their intentions, feelings, and desires—and we lose track of how our words and actions affect them.

Finally, consider love and intimacy. Loving, intimate connections within a caring relationship usually give rise to pleasurable feelings, but if we're cut off from our body, we can't feel or enjoy them. Instead, we feel numb or empty. This makes intimate connection an unpleasant experience, which feeds into *dis*connection and loneliness—and often leads to avoidance of intimacy.

The more you "stay away" from your body, the less access you have to your emotions, so the problems caused by your loss only accumulate. Scientific research shows that "getting back into our bodies" greatly improves our health and well-being (and plays a central role in recovery from trauma). This is why in dropping anchor, you repeatedly acknowledge your feelings and connect with your body. Moving, stretching, breathing, or altering your posture are simple ways to connect with your body.

Mind and Body Working to Help You

So, when your mind and body generate painful thoughts and feelings, they're trying to help you. All that discomfort they generate—all those difficult thoughts, all those fight-and-flight responses, all those painful emotions and feelings, and all that numbness and emptiness—stems from one overarching purpose: your mind and body are working hard to protect you, to save you from getting hurt or harmed.

That's all very well, you may be thinking, *but I still don't like it.* And I agree with you. No one likes pain and discomfort. No one wants it, no one chooses it. Life hit you hard, and your mind and body responded the best way they know how. You didn't ask for all this suffering; life dumped it on you. And it really hurts. And when life hurts this badly, kindness is called for. Running away from our feelings is not a kind way to treat ourselves, because it creates so many problems in the long run. What we need is a radically different way of responding to difficult feelings, which is the focus of our next chapter.

In the meantime, I hope this chapter has encouraged you to start looking at your emotions in a different way. Please keep on noticing and naming them—*Here's sadness, I'm noticing anger, I'm having feelings of guilt,* and so on. At the same time, even if you don't yet fully understand what it is, see if you can also acknowledge that they serve a purpose. You might even silently say to yourself, *These emotions aren't out to get me; they're here to help me.*

10 A Curious Look

A wave of nausea washes over you. Your eyesight becomes blurry and foggy, and within a few seconds, you're blind. Your throat is paralyzed almost instantly, preventing you from speaking or swallowing. Within two to three minutes, this paralysis spreads throughout your body until you can no longer breathe. This is how your life would end if you were bitten by the tiny bird-like beak of the deadly blue-ringed octopus, an organism no bigger than a tennis ball.

My good friend Paddy Spruce likes to ask the question, "If you were swimming near a blue-ringed octopus, would you pick it up, chase it away, ignore it, or simply observe it?" We have all these options available to us, but the first two are deadly, and while this octopus is not naturally aggressive, if you pick it up or threaten it in any way, it will bite. (Just before it attacks, the blue rings on its tentacles suddenly light up.) The third option—ignoring it—would be difficult to do, knowing how deadly it is. Plus, if you don't pay attention to where it is, you might accidentally swim into it.

So the last option, observing it, is clearly the best. *Hang on a minute,* you might be thinking, *there's another option: I could swim away from it.* Yes, you could. However, the blue-ringed octopus prefers to hide under rocks rather than swim in the open, so if you stay still and observe, it will soon pass by and leave you alone. Even if you choose to swim away, wouldn't you first want to look at it, knowing that as long as you didn't try to pick it up or threaten it, you are perfectly safe?

This tiny sea creature provides a good analogy for a painful emotion: if you hold on to it, chase it away, or try to ignore it, the results are usually bad. Many of us treat our emotions as if they were as dangerous as that octopus. We want to get rid of them or avoid them. We're uneasy when they're around. We try to figure out how to make them leave. This attitude, unfortunately, absorbs much of our energy and drains our vitality. However, it doesn't have to be that way. Why? Because unlike the octopus, our feelings are *not* dangerous. If we stay still and observe our emotions with curiosity, then they cannot harm us in any way, and like that blue-ringed octopus, sooner or later they will pass us by.

Now suppose you were a marine biologist and you had paid a small fortune for the opportunity to observe the blue-ringed octopus in its natural environment. Under those circumstances, knowing you were safe, you'd observe that creature with absolute fascination. You'd be curious about its every move. You'd notice the rhythmic movements of its tentacles; you'd notice the beautiful patterns and colors on its body; and you'd respect it as a magnificent work of nature. It's this type of open, curious attention that helps reduce the impact of our emotions.

In other words, when a painful feeling arises, we don't have to get sucked into it nor do we need to fight it or run from it. Instead, we can observe it and allow it to come and go in its own good time. And if your mind responds to that by protesting, threatening, worrying, judging, or resisting in some other way, then please let it have its say—and keep reading.

Feelings, Emotions, and Sensations

Many people get confused about the differences between feelings, emotions, and sensations, so let's clarify a bit. The hardest term to clarify is "feelings," because it's used in so many ways. It's commonly used as another word for emotions—for example, feelings of sadness or anger (I often use it this way). But it's also used for physiological states—feelings of thirst, hunger, sickness, or tiredness. Most commonly, it's used as a synonym for "sensations," meaning anything that we feel in our physical body—whether that's the tightness in our chest when we're anxious, burning in our fingers when we accidentally touch a hot stove, or feelings of numbness when freeze mode kicks in.

The term "emotions" is also hard to clarify because most experts can't completely agree on what they are. But they almost all agree that emotions communicate, motivate, and illuminate, and that physically an emotion includes neurological changes (involving the brain and nervous system), cardiovascular changes (involving the heart and circulatory system), and hormonal changes (involving the "chemical messengers" of the blood). We can measure these changes on scientific instruments, but this isn't how we experience our own emotions. When we look at our emotions with open, curious attention, all we encounter are thoughts and sensations. (Remember: "thoughts" are words and pictures inside our head; "sensations" are what we feel inside our body.)

To make sense of this, check it out: observe your emotions with curiosity. As you do this, you will notice something comprised either of sensations or of words and pictures—or complex, interweaving, multilayered tapestries of pictures, words, and sensations. You can zoom in on specific thoughts or sensations, or you can zoom out and take in the whole spectacle.

To make this clearer, consider your favorite movie. If you were to watch a one-second segment of that film, all you'd see (and hear) are sounds and pictures. We wouldn't call any one of those sounds or pictures a "movie" nor would we say a movie is nothing but sounds and pictures. But, *experientially*, when you take that one-second look, all you will encounter are sounds and pictures. You can think of an emotion similarly: a rich, compelling, multilayered creation comprised of many interweaving sensations and thoughts.

When we pay attention to the threatening, unpleasant, or painful stuff inside us—those thoughts and feelings that we normally turn away from— and take a good honest look at it all and really examine it with openness and curiosity, then we're likely to discover something useful. We learn that this emotion is not as big as it seems and we can make room for it. We learn that it cannot harm us, even though it feels unpleasant. We learn that it cannot control our arms and legs, even though it may make us shiver and shake. We learn that there is no need to run and hide from it, nor to fight and struggle with it. This frees us up to invest time and energy in improving our life rather than in trying to control the way we feel.

Normally, when painful feelings arise, we are not curious about them. We have no desire to get up close, study them, and see what they are comprised of. We have no interest in learning from them. Generally speaking, we don't want to know about them at all. We want to forget them, distract ourselves from them, or get rid of them as fast as possible. We instinctively turn away from them, and yet, as automatic as it is, we can change our response with practice.

Working as a doctor, I have had the opportunity to see many different ways in which the human body can become deformed: through blistering skin diseases, the terrible scarring of burns, the merciless rampages of cancer and AIDS, the distorted swollen joints of immune disorders, the missing limbs that result from surgical amputations, the misshapen heads and twisted spines of rare genetic disorders, the bloated abdomens and yellowing flesh of liver disease, and the myriad forms of physical deterioration associated with old age, illness, and death.

Before I entered the medical profession, I felt a sense of shock, fear, aversion, or disgust whenever I saw people with these conditions. But over the years, I gradually learned to see past the unpleasant exterior and connect with the human being inside. I learned to pay attention with warmth, curiosity, and openness. Over time, my aversion and fear disappeared, and in its place came kindness and compassion. However, this only happened through my willingness to be present and open up; to make room for my automatic emotional reactions without letting them control me. If we are willing, we're all capable of making this transition.

At this point, let's note that there are two very different types of curiosity: a cold, detached, uncaring curiosity, such as that of a lab scientist doing experiments on an animal, and a warm, caring curiosity, such as that of a kindly vet determining how to heal a sick animal. You've probably met doctors who are cold and detached, curious only about the illness, interested only in the diagnosis and treatment. They seem to care very little about the human being inside that afflicted body. And you've probably met other doctors who are warm, kind, and caring in their curiosity. They care about and treat the whole person, not just the condition. Which kind of doctor would you prefer to have treating you?

The word "curiosity" originates from the Latin term *curiosus*, which means "careful" or "diligent." This, in turn, comes from the Latin word *cura*, which means "care." When practicing self-compassion, we care for ourselves—about what we feel and how we respond to our feelings. Avoidance of our feelings is, in contrast, often an uncaring act. We get so focused on getting rid of them that we harm ourselves or shrink our lives in the process. The word *cura* also gives us the word "cure," which seems appropriate because curiosity plays an essential role in emotional healing; instead of escaping from our pain, we turn toward it, investigate it, explore it, and, ultimately, make room for it. This is a true act of caring and healing.

So the next time loneliness, resentment, anxiety, guilt, sadness, anger, or fear shows up, what if you could become really curious about those experiences? What if you could shine a light on them, study them as if they were the prize exhibit in a show?

As we look with more curiosity into any intense stress or discomfort, we'll find that it is comprised of two major components. One is the storyline: the words and pictures inside our heads—beliefs, ideas, assumptions, reasons, rules, judgments, impressions, interpretations, images, and memories. The other is our body sense: the feelings and sensations inside our body, which we'll focus on next.

Making Room

Time for another exercise! We're going to learn how to open up and make room for difficult feelings, but first notice what your mind has to say. Is it enthusiastic, curious, eager, or is it protesting: *No! I want to get rid of these feelings, not make room for them!?*

If the latter, your mind has probably forgotten why we're about to do this important work. Remember chapter 4, where we looked at everything you've done to avoid these feelings, and how that works in the short run but not the long run? How the more effort and energy you expend in avoiding and getting rid of these feelings, the more tired and drained you are, the harder it is to act effectively in the face of all your hardships, and the harder it is to engage in any aspect of life? And remember the last chapter, where we looked at the costs of cutting off from our emotions? Learning how to drop the struggle with your feelings and let them freely flow through you is an act of self-kindness. You're not doing this work just for the sake of it; you're doing it so you can start rebuilding your life.

Before we start the exercise, a few quick reminders. First, if you'd like my voice as a guide, download the audio from the free e-book, *When Life Hits Hard: Extra Bits,* from the Free Resources page on my website, www.the happinesstrap.com, and if you have difficulties with breathing exercises, such as those discussed in chapter 8, then ignore any instruction to do with your breath.

Second, the exercise begins with anchor dropping. That's essential; please don't skip it. And if at any point the exercise becomes overwhelming (I'm not expecting this—just being cautious), then please stop doing it, and drop anchor until you are once again grounded.

Third, it's okay to do this in baby steps. No one expects a firefighter to tackle a towering inferno without any training. The trainee firefighter practices on small, safe fires, lit under carefully controlled conditions within specially designed training grounds. Only when she's practiced a lot, knows her equipment inside out, knows all the drills and maneuvers—only then will she go out and fight real fires.

A similar approach is wise when you make room for difficult feelings. Don't begin with your most overwhelming emotions. Start with those smaller, less challenging feelings: the everyday impatience, frustration, disappointment, sadness, and anxiety. If necessary, start with just one small sensation somewhere in your body, and gradually, over time, work up to bigger ones.

Notice Your Feeling

Take a few moments to drop anchor. Do this in your own manner—acknowledging your inner experience, connecting with your body, engaging in the world around you—until you feel you're grounded.

Then pause for a moment.

You're about to embark on a voyage of discovery—to explore a difficult feeling and see it with new eyes. If no such feeling is present, see if you can bring one up: take a few moments to reflect on the nature of your loss and the way it currently affects you. Usually as you do this, difficult feelings will arise.

Take a slow, gentle breath and focus your attention on your body.

Start at the top of your head and scan downward. Notice where in your body this feeling is strongest: your forehead, eyes, jaw, mouth, throat, neck, shoulders, chest, abdomen, pelvis, buttocks, arms, or legs. (If you're numb, focus on wherever the numbness is most evident: often the chest or abdomen.)

Once you have located a difficult feeling, observe it with wide-eyed curiosity as if you're a marine biologist who has encountered some fascinating new denizen of the deep. See if you can discover something new about it—where it is, what it feels like, or how it behaves.

Notice its energy, pulsation, or vibration. Notice the different "layers" within it.

Notice where it starts and stops.

Is it deep within you or at the surface? Moving or still?

Imagine this feeling as an object inside you: What is its shape and size? Is it light or heavy?

What is its temperature? Can you notice hot spots or cold spots within it?

What is its color? Is it transparent or opaque?

If you could touch the surface of this object, what would it feel like?

Hot or cold? Soft or hard? Rough or smooth?

Notice any resistance you may have to it. Is your body tensing up around it? Is your mind protesting or fretting?

Name Your Feeling

As you notice your feeling, name it. Silently say to yourself, *Here's fear, I'm noticing anger,* or *I'm having a feeling of guilt.* (If you can't pinpoint the exact name of the feeling, then try *Here's pain, Here's stress,* or *Here's numbness.*)

Continue to observe this feeling. Now that it has a name, you know what you're dealing with.

Breathe into Your Feeling

Breathe slowly and deeply, and imagine your breath flowing into and around the emotion.

And as your breath does this, it's as if in some way you expand and a space opens up inside you.

This is the space of awareness.

And just as the ocean has room for all its inhabitants, your own spacious awareness can easily contain all your emotions.

So breathe into the feeling and open around it. Loosen up around it. Give it space.

Breathe into any resistance within your body: the tension, the knots, the contraction, and make space for that too.

Breathe into any resistance from your mind: the smoky haze of *No, Bad,* or *Go away.*

And as you release the breath, also release your thoughts. Instead of holding onto them, let them come and go like leaves in the breeze.

Allow Your Feeling

There is no need to like, want, or approve of this feeling. Just see if you can allow it.

Remember this feeling serves a purpose; your body trying to help you.

This feeling tells you something very important.

It tells you that you care; that you have a heart; that there's something that really matters to you.

It's not a sign of weakness or mental illness. It's a sign that you're a normal, living, caring human being.

Know that you share this feeling with billions of others; we all experience loss and the pain that goes with it.

Can you drop the struggle and make peace with it?

This feeling is a part of you. It's just as much a part of you as your hands and feet, your eyes and ears.

What do you get for battling with parts of yourself? Can you step out of that battle and make peace?

As you continue to observe this feeling, see if there's anything underneath it. For example, if anger or numbness is at the surface, perhaps underneath it is fear, sadness, or shame. Don't try to make a new feeling appear; just allow your feelings to be as they are in this moment. If a new feeling emerges from the deep, that's okay; if it doesn't, that's okay too.

Whatever feeling is present in this moment, let it have its space. Give it plenty of room to move. And allow it to come and go freely, in its own good time.

Expand Your Awareness

Once you've made space for your feeling, the aim is to expand your awareness. Continue to notice your feeling, and at the same time recognize it is only one aspect of this present moment.

Around this feeling is your body, and with that body you can see, hear, touch, taste, and smell.

So step back and admire the view; do not only notice what you're feeling but also what you're hearing, seeing, and touching.

Think of your awareness as the beam of a powerful flashlight, revealing what lies hidden in the darkness. Shine it in all directions, to get a clear sense of where you are.

As you do this, don't try to distract yourself from this feeling. And don't try to ignore it. Keep it in your awareness as you also connect with the world around you.

Allow the feeling to be there, along with everything else that is present.

Notice what you feel and think.

Notice what you are doing and how you are breathing. Notice it all. Take it all in.

Straddle two worlds with your awareness: the one within you and the one outside you. Illuminate both with your consciousness.

And engage fully in life as it is in this moment.

As with all exercises in this book, you can practice this anytime, any-place, for any duration. To improve your ability to make room for difficult emotions, you could stretch this into a long exercise, taking ten to fifteen minutes. Or you can practice a ten- to fifteen-second version just about anywhere: simply notice and name the emotion, breathe into it, allow it to be there, and expand your awareness to connect with the world around you. You can also mix "making room" with other exercises. For example, after noticing, naming, and allowing your feeling, it's great to finish up with some kind self-talk or dropping anchor.

You may be wondering, *What's next? After I finish this practice, what do I do?* The answer is, if you're doing something purposeful and life enhancing, keep doing it and engage in it fully; focus all your attention on it and become thoroughly absorbed in it. And if you're *not* doing something purposeful and life enhancing, then stop and switch to an activity that's more meaningful. (If you can't think of any meaningful activities, we'll get to that in part 2.)

An important reminder: Emotion control strategies—things you do to escape, avoid, or get rid of unwanted feelings—are only problematic if and when you use them excessively, when they're giving you relief in the short run but impairing your life in the long run. So, if they help you cope and don't adversely affect your life in the long run, then keep using them. Here we're giving you more options so you don't have to fight or run from your feelings, or cut off from your body to escape them.

I encourage you to make the effort, at least several times a day, to take a good curious look at your feelings. Watch them closely and discover their habits. When do they appear? What brings them out? Which parts of your body do they like to occupy? And how does your body react to them? Where do you notice resistance, tension, and struggle?

When watching a documentary, we can be thrilled at the sight of a shark, crocodile, or stingray. These deadly creatures fill us with awe and appreciation. Our challenge is to view our emotions in the same way. Although our feelings might appear to be dangerous, they are actually unable to harm us in any way. Unlike a shark or a crocodile, they cannot eat us. Unlike a stingray, they cannot poison us. So, when we watch our feelings with openness and curiosity, it's no more dangerous than watching a wildlife documentary. So take a curious look, whenever you can. It doesn't have to be a long look, just a curious one.

11   A Kind Hand

You've got a pet donkey, right? And every weekend, your donkey carries your goods to the marketplace for you to sell there. No? Oh. Oh well, never mind. Even if you don't have a donkey, I'm sure you know that donkeys are renowned for being stubborn. So if you want your donkey to cooperate, you need to know how to motivate it. And if you're wondering what on earth this has to do with loss, you'll find out very shortly.

Often our losses are forced upon us, through death, disease, or disaster. At other times, we contribute to our losses, at least in part, through our own self-defeating behavior. We all screw up, get it wrong, and make foolish mistakes. We all, at times, get jerked around by our emotions like a puppet on a string and act in self-defeating ways. Struggling with our thoughts and feelings, we say and do things that are far removed from the person we really want to be. We hurt the people we love the most, or we avoid them because we feel unworthy of their love.

As we practice and apply the principles within this book, we'll find this sort of thing happens less often, but we'll never be perfect. We'll screw up again and again because we're human.

So what does your mind tend to do when you screw up? If it's like my mind, it pulls out a big stick and starts whacking you; it tells you you're not good enough, you can't do it, or there's something wrong with you; or it lectures you about trying harder, doing better, and improving yourself. This is hardly surprising, because as children, adults often criticized us to get us to change our behavior; it's no wonder then that we learned to do this to ourselves.

Now back to that donkey I mentioned earlier. You've probably heard the old saying about "carrot versus stick." If you want a donkey to carry your load, you can motivate it with a carrot or a stick. Both approaches get the donkey moving but, over time, the more you hit that donkey with the stick, the more miserable and unhealthy it becomes. But if you reward the donkey with a carrot whenever it does what you want, then over time you end up with a much healthier donkey.

Beating yourself up is just as ineffective as hitting a donkey with a stick. Sure, self-criticism sometimes gets you moving in the right direction, but the more habitual it becomes, the more miserable and unhealthy you will be. It's highly unlikely to change your behavior; it's more likely to keep you feeling stuck and miserable. So whether our loss came about by sheer bad luck or whether we in some way contributed to it, practicing self-compassion is essential.

By the way, the skills you've learned—dropping anchor, unhooking from unhelpful stories, making room for difficult emotions—are known as "mindfulness skills." Because mindfulness is a big part of ACT, you may wonder why I haven't mentioned it before. The reason is simply because there are so many false notions about mindfulness; people think it's a religious practice, a type of meditation, a relaxation technique, or a form of positive thinking. None of those ideas is correct. "Mindfulness" has many different definitions, and there's no universal agreement as to which definition is best.

Personally, I define *mindfulness* as a set of psychological skills for effective living, which all involve paying attention with openness, curiosity, and flexibility. When we drop anchor, unhook from unhelpful stories, and make room for difficult emotions, we are responding *flexibly* to our experience, *paying attention* to what is present with an attitude of *openness* and *curiosity*; in other words, we are practicing mindfulness.

Of course, some people are more mindful than others: more able to focus on and engage in what they are doing, to open up and make room for their feelings, and to unhook from their thoughts. This is largely due to the amount of practice they do. So far, I've only spoken about informal practice: quick and simple mindfulness exercises you can readily do throughout the day, virtually anytime, anyplace. However, if you'd like to really develop your capacity for mindfulness, you may also want to consider a formal practice, such as mindfulness meditation, Hatha yoga, or tai chi.

One particular formal practice, which I highly recommend, is very useful: mindfulness of the breath. It involves focusing attention on your breathing and bringing your attention back repeatedly, no matter how often it wanders. Appendix B offers a detailed description of the exercise. However, if you've never done a practice like this, you'll be shocked at how challenging it is. If you can focus on your breath for even ten seconds before your attention wanders, you'll be doing well.

All the mindfulness skills we've covered so far are important elements of self-compassion; they are kind ways of responding to your loss and handling painful thoughts, feelings, and memories. Now we will blend these mindfulness skills together, along with some kind words and kind actions, to give you the full experience of self-compassion. (An audio version is available in my free e-book *When Life Hits Hard: Extra Bits*. See the Free Resources page on my website, www.thehappinesstrap.com.) Some clients, especially men, are initially reluctant to do this next exercise; they protest that it's "silly," "flowery," or "touchy-feely." But once they try it, they usually find it helpful. (Antonio certainly did, as you'll see.)

A Kind Hand

Find a comfortable position in which you are centered and alert. For example, if you're seated in a chair, you could lean slightly forward, straighten your back, drop your shoulders, and press your feet gently into the floor.

Take a few moments to drop anchor. Do this in your own manner—acknowledging your inner experience, connecting with your body, engaging in the world around you—until you have a sense that you're grounded.

Now bring to mind your loss. Take a few moments to reflect on what has happened, and notice what thoughts and feelings arise.

1.   Be Present.

Pause.

That's all you need do—just pause.

Pause for a few seconds and notice what your mind is telling you. Notice its choice of words, and the speed and volume of its speech.

Be curious: is this story old and familiar, or is it something new? Is your mind taking you into the past, present, or future? What judgments is it making? What labels is it using?

Don't try to debate with your mind or try to silence it; you'll only stir it up.

Simply notice the story it's telling you.

And notice, with curiosity, all the different feelings that arise in your body. What do you discover? Guilt, sadness, anger, fear, or embarrassment? Resentment, despair, anguish, rage, or anxiety? Numbness, emptiness, apathy? Pay attention, like a curious child, to what is going on inside your body.

Name these feelings as they arise: *Here's fear, Here's sadness, Here's numbness.*

Say something compassionate to yourself: acknowledge your pain and respond with kindness. If you're not sure what to say, try, *This is difficult. Hold yourself kindly.*

2.   Open Up.

Now find the feeling that bothers you the most and observe it like a curious child.

Where is it located? Is it at the surface or deep inside?

What is its size and shape? Are its borders well defined, or vague and fuzzy?

What's the temperature of this feeling? Can you notice any hot spots or cold spots within it?

Is it moving or still? Light, heavy, or weightless?

Can you notice any other sensations within it? Vibrating, tingling, or throbbing? Pressure, burning, or cutting?

Now slowly and gently breathe into the feeling, with an attitude of warmth and kindness.

Imagine your breath flowing into and around this pain or numbness.

Imagine that, in some magical way, a vast space opens up inside you, making plenty of room for this difficult feeling.

No matter how unwanted this feeling may be, do not fight it. Step out of the battle. Instead, make peace with it.

Let this feeling be as it is. Give it plenty of space rather than pushing it away.

And if you notice any resistance in your body—tightening, contraction, or tension—breathe into that too. Make room for it.

Make space for all that arises: your thoughts, your feelings, and your resistance.

3.   Hold Yourself Kindly.

Now choose one of your hands.

Imagine this is the hand of someone very kind and caring.

Place this hand, slowly and gently, either on your heart or on the feeling. If you don't wish to touch your body, let your hand hover above the area where the feeling is.

Do you feel this more in your chest, or perhaps in your head, neck, or stomach? Wherever it bothers you most, lay your hand there. (If you can't locate any particular place, rest or hover your hand over your heart.)

Let your hand rest there, lightly and gently.

Sense its warmth flowing into your body.

Imagine your body softening around the pain, loosening up, and making space.

Hold this pain or numbness gently. Hold it as if it is a crying baby, a whimpering puppy, or a fragile work of art.

Infuse this gentle action with caring and warmth, as if reaching out to support someone you care about.

Let the kindness flow from your fingers.

Now, use both of your hands. Place one of them on your chest and the other on your stomach, and let them gently rest there. Hold yourself kindly and gently: connecting with yourself, caring for yourself, giving comfort and support.

4.   Speak Kindly.

Now say a few kind words to yourself.

If you're not sure what to say, try, *This is difficult; hold yourself kindly.*

Or you might say, *This is difficult—and I can do this.*

If you've failed or made a mistake, then you might like to remind yourself, *Yes, I'm human. Like everybody else, I fail and make mistakes.*

Acknowledge that your pain tells you something very important.

It tells you that you have a heart, you care, and you've lost something or someone that really matters to you.

This is what all humans feel in the face of great loss.

It's not a sign of weakness or of something wrong with you; it's a sign that you're a living, caring being. And it's something you have in common with every living, caring being on the planet.

As Antonio did this exercise with me, a guttural growl of anguish broke from his throat. His body heaved, and tears poured down his face. I asked him gently to keep his hands on his body, to continue sending in kindness. And he did. He stayed that way for a good ten minutes, sobbing, shaking, and holding himself kindly. Eventually, his crying stopped and he became calm. He looked at me sheepishly, and said in a hushed voice, "I've been trying so f###ing hard not to feel that."

"And now, how do you feel?"

"Like I just had ten kinds of shit kicked out of me!"

"You seem a lot calmer," I said. The angst and tension he'd brought into the session had evaporated; he looked peaceful.

"Yeah—I guess I am," he said, and smiled.

Antonio's reaction to the kind hand exercise was dramatic. For most people, that doesn't happen. More commonly, you'll tap into a sense of warmth and comfort. It's soothing and calming, and tends to center and quiet you. If you do tap into some strong painful emotions, there's a choice to make. You can end the exercise and drop anchor, or keep going and "ride the storm." Then, when the storm eventually subsides, you'll likely be in a similar state to Antonio; you'll feel like you've been through a lot—perhaps a bit shaky or vulnerable—but you'll also feel calm or comforted.

I encourage you to do this exercise repeatedly—at least daily (but even weekly is beneficial). If it feels too long, strip it down into a two-minute version. It's best to do this in private. It's also great to do in bed, especially if you can't sleep. If you didn't get much out of it, please try it at least one more time. With repetition, most people find it helpful. (However, if you don't want to do it, if you don't get anything out of it, or if it triggers a negative reaction that's too overwhelming for you to handle—just leave it.)

Feel free to adapt or modify this exercise. For example, if you don't like placing your hands as suggested above, substitute another gesture of kindness, such as rubbing your neck or shoulders, or massaging your temples or eyelids.

Going Further

Besides practicing this exercise, what other acts of kindness can you do for yourself? How about making time for your favorite pastime? How about playing sports, tinkering with your car, reading books, or working out in the gym? Having a soothing bath? Getting a massage? Eating some delicious healthy food? Going for a walk? Giving yourself some "me time"? Listening to your favorite music?

We've touched a few times on kind self-talk, and I want to explore this further. As you know, there's no delete button in the brain; we can't magically eliminate all those harsh self-judgmental thoughts. In ACT, we don't challenge, dispute, try to disprove, or get rid of those self-critical thoughts; we don't turn "negative" thoughts into "positive" ones. Instead we acknowledge the judgmental thoughts, allow them to be present—*and in addition* we bring in kind self-talk; we speak to ourselves the way we would to a good friend in need.

For example, suppose your mind says, *I'm so weak. Why can't I be stronger? Why can't I handle this as well as other people?* You might respond, *I'm noticing thoughts about being weak. This really hurts, and I'm struggling—but even though it's difficult, I can handle this. I'll take it one day at a time and focus on what's in my control.*

Or suppose your mind says you are a bad person because you weren't there for a loved one, you weren't able to save them from something bad, or you treated them badly—and it makes nasty self-judgments. You might respond, *Here's* The I Screwed Up Story. *Yes, I regret lots of things. I wish I could go back and do things differently—and it really hurts that I can't. But beating myself up won't change what happened. What I can do, though, is learn from this, so I can act differently if something similar ever happens again.*

Notice in these responses, there's no self-pity or attempt to deny or dismiss your very real pain. There's no trite positive thinking: "If life gives you lemons, make lemonade" or "Look at the glass half full." They all elaborate on that basic two-step formula: acknowledge your pain, respond with kindness.

Of course, this is a lot easier said than done: as with any new skill, self-compassion takes practice. But also, it does get easier with practice. So, throughout each day, find opportunities to notice and name your harsh, self-judgmental thoughts and allow them to be present. Then consider: How would you be kind and supportive to a loved one experiencing a hard loss? What would you say? Then say something similar to yourself.

Think Small

To develop self-compassion, we don't have to do something big and dramatic. The tiniest act of kindness makes a difference. For example, here are a few kind acts I did this morning: I stretched my back and neck, took a hot shower, played with the dog, joked around with my son, ate a healthy breakfast, and listened to the birds outside the window. Such tiny acts of caring build up over time into a supportive, compassionate relationship with yourself. And even if you just *imagine* doing these acts, then that in itself can generate a sense of self-kindness.

Earlier I mentioned Kristin Neff, the world's top researcher on self-compassion. Neff identifies three core elements of self-compassion. The first two are mindfulness and kindness. The third is called "common humanity," which refers to the human condition and the universal nature of suffering. When we are hurting and suffering, let's remind ourselves that these are *normal* human experiences; that all over the planet, in this moment, millions upon millions of human beings are suffering in ways similar to our own. We don't do this to discount or trivialize our pain, but rather to acknowledge it as part of being human, as something we have in common with everyone else, as something that can help us to understand the suffering of others and extend our compassion to them too.

Often when we're suffering, our mind tells us that we are the only one who suffers and everyone else is happier than we are! If we buy this story, it makes our suffering all the more intense. The reality is that all humans suffer, and loss and hardship touch every human life, often many times. As part of our kind self-talk, it can be useful to remind ourselves of this.

Personally, I find self-compassion hardest on those occasions when I have yelled at my son. Like all parents, at times I lose my temper. Hooked by some judgmental story, I lose touch with my values of patience and calmness, and I snap and say harsh words. Moments later, my mind comes out with the big stick: *Bad father! What a lousy job you're doing! He's just a kid, go easy on him; what are you losing your temper for? Call yourself an ACT therapist? What a hypocrite you are! What would the readers think if they could see you now?* Before I know it, I am flailing around in an emotional storm of guilt, embarrassment, and frustration.

And then…after a while…I realize what's going on. I plant my feet into the floor, take some deep breaths, and notice what I can see, hear, touch, taste, and smell. I connect with the world; I become present. And I acknowledge that I am hurting. Then I gently place a hand on my chest or my abdomen—wherever it hurts the most—and breathe deeply. I remind myself: *You're a human being. And like every other parent on the planet, you screw up sometimes. This is what it feels like when you really care about being a good parent and you don't manage to live up to your own ideals.*

And then I look deeper at what's underneath all that guilt. And there it is: LOVE. Sheer, boundless love. After all, if I didn't love him, I wouldn't feel guilty about yelling at him.

So, if you make the time to sit quietly, to be kind and gentle with your-self, and take a curious look at your emotional pain, then I suspect you will find something similar inside you. Whatever the emotion is—anger, fear, sadness, or guilt—hold it gently and ask yourself, *What does this pain reveal about my heart? What is it reminding me of that I really care about? What does it tell me that I need to face up to, deal with, or do differently?*

These questions help you to remember that you are not "bad," even if your mind says you are. You are a caring human being. After all, if you didn't care, you wouldn't hurt.

So when life hits hard and our world falls apart, dropping anchor and holding ourselves kindly help us to regroup after the blow, to get back on our feet and collect ourselves. After that, we'll be far more effective when we move into strategizing and problem solving: taking action, guided by our values, to start the painful process of rebuilding. So throughout your day, in addition to repeatedly dropping anchor, look for opportunities to practice tiny acts of self-kindness. Each and every one of them makes a difference.

When Memories Hurt

Sometimes the sweetest, richest memories give rise to the most painful emotions. This is especially so when we've lost someone we love through death, separation, or relationship breakdown. As we remember the good times—those moments of love and play, intimacy and connection, sharing and caring—the enormity of our loss confronts us. All of a sudden, that sweet joyful memory is awash with sadness, anxiety, loneliness, or other painful feelings. And those are the good memories! With bad memories, we suffer even more because there's no love or sweetness in them—only more pain.

In this chapter, we'll look at two different yet somewhat connected strategies. First, we'll explore "grieving practices" for working with the pain of good memories and then "giving exercises" for coping with the pain of bad ones.

Groundwork Already Laid

The good news is that you've already done some solid groundwork for what comes next. You've been dropping anchor when painful memories show up, an excellent first step for any painful inner experience. You've also noticed and named them: *I'm noticing a memory of the funeral, I'm having a memory of the car accident, I notice my mind remembering how she held me, Here's a memory of my boss sacking me.*

You've also been using kind self-talk—acknowledging how painful the memory is and responding with kindness. You've made room for painful feelings and unhooked from self-judgmental stories: *I'm having the thought that I screwed up, Here's my mind telling me that I'm weak, I'm noticing* The Damaged Goods Story.

Hopefully, these practices have already made a big difference, and you've noticed that your memories come and go in their own good time. (If you haven't been practicing these things, now is a great time to start.) Now let's build on those skills.

Practices for Acknowledging Loss

When someone you love dies, practices for acknowledging loss (also known as "grief rituals") are usually of great value. (We'll talk shortly about modifying these exercises for other types of loss.) Basically, you create a routine or ceremony that you do regularly to help you, over time, come to terms with your loss. There are no firm rules about how to do this (e.g., how long to do it for or how often); you need to experiment to discover what's best for you. Many people find it helpful to include most or all of the following elements.

A Regular Time and Place

Many people find it very comforting to do this practice regularly: same time (daily, weekly, monthly), same place. You might visit a graveyard, go to a beach or forest, visit a place of worship, or use a room in your house. You might take five minutes, an hour, or half a day. Find what works for you.

A Strong Reminder

It's often helpful to have something present that strongly reminds you of your loved one. This can be a photograph or painting, an item of their clothing, a toy or teddy bear they loved.

A Symbolic Act

Do something that symbolizes your love for this person—light a candle, lay flowers on a grave, play special music, read a poem, pray, or journal. If another person participates, you might hold their hand, hug them, or sing or pray together.

Remembering and Allowing

During this time, remember your loved one and allow your feelings to be as they are. Make room for all your thoughts and feelings: love and sadness, joy and fear, laughter and loneliness. Acknowledge how much it hurts, and treat yourself kindly. Many people find it soothing to practice the kind hands exercise from chapter 11.

Remember that unwanted memories may appear. If this happens, it's important that you don't push them away, because doing so usually results in a rebound effect: the unwanted memories disappear briefly, then bounce back with a vengeance. So if an unwanted memory shows up, notice it, name it, allow it—and hold yourself kindly.

Choosing Memories

We have little control over our memories. They come and go as they please. Often they appear when we don't want them; at other times, we can't retrieve them, no matter how we try. However, during a grieving ritual, you can choose to focus on memories that you want to hold dear. Consider how you want to remember this person: Were there particular occasions or events that were really special? Things they said or did that really mattered to you? Quirks of their personality you found endearing? Personal qualities you admired? If so, you may like to consciously relive and reflect on these beautiful moments, and savor the sweetness within them.

Talking with Your Loved One

And finally, many people find it useful to talk to their loved one. If you've never done this, it might sound odd, because your loved one is dead. Yet these imaginary conversations are often very healing. If you want to experiment with this, you may choose to speak aloud or in your head. You may like to talk to your loved one about old times, tell them things you wish you'd said, or keep them informed of what's happening now in your life. If you wish, you can imagine them talking back to you.

Natalie, whose son died in the hit-and-run, was quite religious. She had a twice-weekly practice of visiting her son's grave—and during those visits, she prayed, spoke to him, and laid flowers on his tombstone. In addition, every night she would light a candle in his bedroom and pick up an item of his clothing. She would practice the kind hands exercise—holding the clothing against her body, underneath her hands—and let herself cry. Then she'd finish up with a prayer.

Antonio and Cathy created a practice where once a week they'd go into baby Sophia's bedroom, stand in front of her crib, and hold hands. They'd light a candle, play music, and share with each other their fondest memories of their beautiful baby girl. Usually they'd end up sobbing and hugging each other tightly.

It's hard to overestimate the power of these kinds of practices. They are not for everyone (it's fine if you skip them), but most people find them very comforting—even though they're often very painful. Because of that, it's a good idea to begin with dropping anchor, and to bring it in again as often as needed. And like everything else in this book, experiment and find what works for you.

For other types of loss—job, health, or an important relationship—these practices can also be useful, but usually they're low key. For example, Shanti's practice, following the breakup of her marriage, was to sit on the couch for ten minutes every night, acknowledge her heartbreak, make room for all the memories that surfaced, and practice the kind hands exercise. Rada's practice—acknowledging all that she had lost because of her chronic illness—was almost identical to Shanti's, except she did it in the morning before getting out of bed.

"Giving Support" Exercises

How do we deal with really awful memories—memories loaded with threat, danger, violence, death, disaster? All those skills we discussed in the "Groundwork Already Laid" section earlier are very important. If you've been practicing them, you've probably found that the impact of these awful memories has lessened. "Giving support" exercises offer a way to reduce that impact even further. These are essentially exercises in imagination. You imagine yourself traveling back in time to soon after the bad event happened, and then you imagine giving yourself the support you didn't have at that time.

For example, the first time he did this, Antonio imagined himself traveling back to the day after the death of baby Sophia. In his imagination, the Antonio of now stood beside the Antonio back then, placed an arm around his shoulders, and spoke to him in a kind and comforting manner.

Emily had been in a horrific car accident that crushed her pelvis and scarred her legs. She imagined that the Emily of now traveled back in time to give support to the Emily back then (four months prior), arriving at the moment she was finally removed from the mangled car. The Emily of now comforted the Emily back then, held her hand in the ambulance, and stayed by her bedside in the hospital.

Note that in these exercises, *you don't go back to the actual awful event.* The reason for this is that it's often too overwhelming to do this alone. If you're having flashbacks or extremely distressing memories, find a well-trained therapist who is skilled in a process called "exposure," which involves working directly with the memories, with lots of guidance and support from the therapist.

Instead of going back to the actual event, you go back to sometime *after* it occurred. And once there, you give yourself support in any way you want. Most people use compassionate words and gestures, but it's your imagination, so you can do whatever you like—as long as it's kind and supportive.

I'm going to take you through one of these giving support exercises now, but please—*don't* work with your current loss. You're not yet ready for it. The aim now is to learn what's involved by working with a memory from a long time ago. After that, you can try this with something more recent. (If you want my voice to guide you, download the free audio from *When Life Hits Hard: Extra Bits.* See the Free Resources page on my website, www.the happinesstrap.com.)

As usual, this exercise begins with dropping anchor. If ever something overwhelming happens (not expecting it—just being cautious), please stop the exercise and drop anchor.

Giving Support to the Younger You

You are about to do an exercise in imagination. Some people imagine with vivid, colorful pictures; others imagine with vague, fuzzy, unclear pictures; and still others imagine without using pictures at all, relying more on words and ideas. However you imagine is just fine.

You're going to imagine traveling back in time to visit a younger version of yourself, at some point in your life when you were struggling, and the people around you were unable to give you the care and support you needed. This could be when you were a child, a teenager, or young adult.

Find a comfortable position and spend a few moments dropping anchor: acknowledging what's going on in your inner world; connecting with your body through moving, stretching, or breathing; and engaging in the world around you: noticing what you can see, hear, and touch.

Once you're grounded, either close your eyes or fix your gaze on a spot, and allow yourself to imagine.

Imagine getting into a time machine in which you travel back in time to visit your younger self. Find the "younger you," who is struggling—and the adults around them, for one reason or another, are not providing the care and support they need.

Step out of the time machine and make contact with the younger you. Take a good look at this person and get a sense of what he is going through. Is she crying? Is he angry or frightened? Does she feel guilty or ashamed? What does this young person really need: love, kindness, understanding, forgiveness, acceptance?

In a kind, calm, and gentle voice, tell this younger you that you know what has happened, that you know what he's been through, that you know how much she is hurting.

Tell this younger you that he doesn't need anyone else to validate that experience because *you* know.

Tell this younger you that she got through this difficult patch in her life, and it is now a distant memory.

Tell this younger you that you are here, that you know how much this truly hurts, and you want to help in any way you can.

Ask this young person if there's anything she needs or wants from you—and whatever she asks for, give it to her. If he asks you to take him somewhere special, go ahead and do it. Offer a hug, a kiss, kind words, or a gift of some sort. This is an exercise in imagination, so you can give her anything she wants. If this younger you doesn't know what he wants or doesn't trust you, then let him know that's fine; he doesn't need to say or do anything.

Tell this young person anything you think he needs to hear to help him understand what has happened—and, if he's been blaming himself, to help him stop doing so.

Tell her that you are here for her, that you care, and you'll do whatever you can to help her get through this.

Continue to radiate caring and kindness toward this younger you in any way you can think of: through words, gestures, deeds—or, if you prefer, through magic or telepathy.

Once you have a sense that this younger you has accepted your caring and kindness, it's time to bid farewell. Give him a gift of some sort to symbolize the connection between you. This may be a toy or teddy bear for a younger child; for someone older, perhaps it's an item of clothing, a book, a magical object, or anything else that springs to mind.

Say good-bye and let her know that you'll come back to visit her again. Then get in your time machine and come back to the present.

Now drop anchor for a minute or so. Acknowledge what's showing up inside you. Connect with your body—have a good long stretch. Engage with the world around you: use your eyes and ears, and notice where you are and what you're doing.

I hope you found that exercise helpful. Now that you know what's involved, you can adapt it to your most recent loss. Like Antonio and Emily, you can go back and visit yourself in the hours, days, weeks, months (or even years) that followed the event. It's often helpful to do this regularly; indeed, on each occasion you do it, you might choose to visit a different point in time.

Please play around with these practices, both of which are infused with self-compassion. Adapt and modify them to suit your unique situation. If they aren't helpful, then skip them. Instead, keep noticing, naming, and dropping anchor whenever painful memories arise. There's no "delete button" in the brain; no way to eliminate painful memories, but over time, as you treat yourself kindly and allow your memories to be present without a struggle, you're likely to notice two things: they'll appear less often, and they'll steadily lose their impact.

This brings us to the end of part 1. Before moving on to part 2, take a few weeks to really work on the skills we've covered so far:

- dropping anchor amid emotional storms

- opening up and making room for difficult feelings

- unhooking from harsh self-talk

- acknowledging your pain and responding with kindness

To regroup after a loss usually is neither quick nor simple. The greater the loss, the deeper the wounds—and deep wounds don't heal quickly. Emotional storms will continue to arise, your mind will continue to tell you unhelpful stories, and you will often forget everything we've covered so far in this book. But...you can get better at remembering, and when you remember, you have a choice: you can, if you wish, drop anchor, acknowledge your pain, and respond to yourself with kindness. And each and every time you make that choice...a little healing happens.

PART
TWO

Rebuild

13　Making Life Meaningful

Without any sense of meaning, life lacks color and richness. It's like living in black and white. There's little or no joy or satisfaction. The odd thing about major losses is that they either fill our lives with meaning—reminding us of what truly matters, connecting us deeply with our heart—or they drain it all away, leaving us empty and dissatisfied. Too often it's the latter, at least during the immediate aftermath. So our aim in part 2, Rebuild, is to turn that around. If your mind says that's impossible, that's a perfectly natural reaction. It takes time, effort, and courage—and much patience—to rebuild your life after a loss.

The harder life hits us, the less motivated we are to think about rebuilding. We're often so exhausted and drained that we dread taking action, so it's important to go slow and think small. Have you ever built a brick wall? No, me neither. But I'm sure you've seen bricklayers in action: they don't simultaneously lay twenty different bricks. They lay one brick at a time. The same principle applies to rebuilding your life. You don't work on every aspect of your life simultaneously; that's a recipe for feeling overwhelmed and hopeless. Instead, focus on one small aspect of life at a time.

What's the Point?

Every action we take serves a purpose—from doing the washing to eating ice cream; from getting married to completing a tax return; from zoning out in front of late-night TV to going for a morning jog. Underlying each and every action is an intention—we're taking action to make something happen. But how often are we conscious of this intention? And how often do our actions *consciously* serve some greater purpose that matters to us?

For most of us, the answer to both questions is "not too often." We tend to go through life on autopilot rather than consciously choosing what we do and how we do it. As a result, we may spend big chunks of our days acting in ways that are largely unfulfilling. However, if we consciously align our actions to a cause that is personally important, then everything changes. Our life becomes imbued with meaning. We develop a sense of direction by behaving like the person we want to be. And we experience a sense of vitality that is wholly missing from life on autopilot.

In the ACT model, this process of making life meaningful is called "living by your values." *Values* are basically your heart's deepest desires for how you want to behave as a human being. They describe what sort of person you want to be, how you want to treat yourself, others, and the world around you. They are like an inner compass that guides you through the winding journey of life. They provide energy that motivates and inspires you to do what matters, even when you don't feel like it.

The next exercise will help you think about your values. But first, it's important to know there are not "right values" or "wrong values." It's like your taste in ice cream. If your favorite flavor is chocolate but someone else prefers vanilla, that doesn't mean that their taste in ice cream is right and yours is wrong, or vice versa. It simply means you have different tastes. Similarly, we all have different values.

Values

This exercise involves simply reading a list of forty common values, ones that many people share. Read the list and see if any of these resonate with you. (Perhaps all or none of them will resonate. It's not a test—just an exercise to get you thinking about values.) Read the list slowly, and pause for 2 seconds after each word to consider if it describes how you would like to behave toward yourself, others, or the world around you, if you could choose to do so.

I'd like to behave in ways that are:

Accepting	Focused	Playful
Adventurous	Friendly	Reliable
Assertive	Forgiving	Respectful
Authentic	Fun loving	Responsible
Attentive	Generous	Self-caring
Caring	Genuine	Self-protective
Committed	Grateful	Self-supportive
Compassionate	Helpful	Sincere
Cooperative	Honest	Supportive
Courageous	Humorous	Trusting
Creative	Kind	Trustworthy
Curious	Loving	Understanding
Engaged	Mindful	
Fair	Open	

If some words describe how you'd like to treat yourself, others, or the world around you, then in the ACT model, we'd call them your "values." (If some words *don't* describe how you want to behave, then they aren't your values—and that's okay.)

Upon the vast table of our life, we find many different dishes—some exquisitely pleasurable, others are intensely painful. When life hits us hard, pleasurable dishes are removed and painful ones replace them. Of course, we want to get rid of all those painful dishes: those difficult problems and agonizing thoughts, feelings, and memories. We want to sweep them off the table and bring back all those precious items we've lost. Unfortunately, we can't do that. So what can we do?

Well, this is where values are useful. Think of your values as what you want to bring to the table of life. Do you want to bring love, courage, kindness? Do you want to bring playfulness, openness, curiosity? Do you want to bring honesty, humor, helpfulness? You can bring these things to the table through your words, actions, and gestures. You can't magically change what life has dished out for you, but you can add to what's on the table, and as you do that, the dishes already there will be transformed.

You've already experienced this in part 1. Life served up many painful thoughts, feelings, and memories—and what you brought to the table was kindness, caring, and compassion. Do those words—kindness, caring, compassion—describe how, deep in your heart, you want to treat yourself and others? If so, you can think of them as your values.

Values versus Goals

Values and goals are radically different, which confuses most of us. This is because we live in a goal-focused society, not a values-focused one. Often when people use the word "values," they are actually talking about "goals." Here's the difference: Values describe *how you want to behave*, while goals describe *what you want to get*. If you want to get a great job, buy a big house, find a partner, get married, or have kids, those are all goals. They can all be checked off the "to do" list: "Goal achieved!" Values, in contrast, are how you want to behave as you move toward your goals, achieve your goals, and even when you *don't* achieve your goals!

For example, if your values are to be loving, kind, and caring, then you can behave in these ways right now and forever—even if you never achieve the goal of, say, finding a partner or having kids. If in the workplace, your values are to be productive, efficient, sociable, attentive, and responsible, you can behave in these ways right now even if your job totally sucks.

Now suppose you want to be loved or respected—are those values? No, they're goals! They're about trying to *get* something—in this case, love or respect from others. Your values are how you want to *behave* as you pursue those goals, whether you achieve them or not. If you want to be loving or respectful, those *are* values; you can act lovingly or respectfully to yourself or others whenever you choose to. But to be loved or respected are goals (some people call them "needs"), and they are out of our control; we can't make someone love us or respect us. But if we act lovingly and respectfully toward ourselves and others, there's a good chance we will be loved and respected in return.

Both values and goals are important, but we need to keep in mind their differences. The easiest way to remember the difference is goals describe what I want to have, get, or achieve; values describe how I want to treat myself, others, or the world around me. And what has all this got to do with loss? Well, once we have regrouped through dropping anchor and self-compassion, the next step is to take action, to stand for something in the face of all our pain. So when life asks, "What will you stand for in the face of this great loss?" the answer lies in our values: "I will stand for being the sort of person I want to be, for acting on what matters, deep in my heart." Through this response, we give ourselves something to live for—a cause or a purpose. We literally give our life meaning.

If this still doesn't make much sense to you, or you get the concept but you're not quite sure what your own values are...then yes, you guessed it, that's normal. When I first talk to people about meaning, purpose, or values, they often become anxious or confused, or go blank, so I take them through a couple of exercises to help them get the hang of it. The first one involves extracting the "hidden wisdom" buried beneath harsh self-judgment.

How's Your Mind Trying to Help?

Begin this exercise by taking a few moments to drop anchor.

Now recall some harsh self-judgments your mind keeps telling you.

Take a moment to name this story or pattern—perhaps "self-judgment," or The Not Good Enough Story, or the "inner critic."

Now consider, when your mind judges you, how's it trying to help?

Is it trying to help you learn from the past?

Is it trying to solve a problem, prepare you for something, or make a plan?

Is it trying to save you from, protect you from, or prepare you for something in the future?

Is it connecting you with someone or something that matters?

Is it reminding you to take care of yourself or someone else?

What's it trying to help you do differently or better?

What personal qualities is it trying to bring out in you?

Natalie's mind had been really getting stuck, calling her a *bad mother* in many different ways. The morning her son died, they'd had a heated argument, and she'd harshly called him selfish and lazy. Those were the last words she ever spoke to him. She'd had various versions of The Bad Mother

Story for many years, but now her mind was really doing a hatchet job—replaying the entire back-catalog of all the times she'd let her son down or treated him unkindly. She'd been dropping anchor, naming the story, making room, practicing kind self-talk and the kind hand exercise, as well as doing her regular grieving rituals, and this had been very helpful—but still her mind kept mercilessly beating her up.

As I took Natalie through the questions above, she had some interesting answers. Obviously, her mind was connecting her with her deep, deep love for her son and wanting her to be a "good" mother instead of a "bad" one.

"So, according to your mind," I asked, "what are the qualities of a 'good mother'?" With a bit of prompting, Natalie identified qualities such as being loving, kind, forgiving, supportive, reliable.

"And those things are important to you? Deep in your heart, that's the sort of mother you want to be?"

"Yes!" she cried. "But it's too late for that! He's dead."

Through reflecting on the questions above, Natalie had tapped into some very important values. And, of course, she was right. Her son was dead, and she could not go back and change the past.

So I asked, "These values of yours—being loving, kind, forgiving, supportive, reliable—are they only for that one relationship, your relationship with Richard? Or are there other people in your life that you'd like to treat that way?"

"Of course there are," she replied. "My husband, my daughter, my friends, my parents…"

"So is this what your mind is trying to help you with? To bring more of those values into your other relationships? Obviously that won't bring Richard back or change the past or get rid of your pain, but could there be something in it that's meaningful for you?" A glimmer of hope flickered across Natalie's face.

With Rada, the process was trickier. Because of her chronic illness (fibromyalgia), Rada had abandoned many activities she had previously enjoyed, such as Latin dancing and aerobics, but her greatest loss was a rather unusual pastime. Rada loved to make abstract sculptures out of wood, clay, and steel. Unfortunately, sculpting is physically strenuous, and the pain in Rada's arms, back, and neck made it impossible. Because of this, Rada's mind kept calling her *pathetic, weak, useless,* and *worthless.*

"I can't see how my mind is trying to help me," she said.

We'd spoken before about the two ways to motivate a donkey—carrot and stick—so I said, "I think your mind is using the big stick method— beating you up to try to get you to do something. What do you think it wants you to do?"

"To start dancing, sculpting, and doing all the things I used to do."

"Yes, I think so too."

"But I can't do those things anymore!" cried Rada.

"That's right. At least for now, you can't. So although your mind wants to help, it's actually getting in the way. First, it's using the big stick, and second, it's pushing you into doing things that aren't currently realistic. So how about you put down the stick and let's look at what *is* realistic for you, given the limitations imposed by your health?"

Rada agreed to do this, so our next step was to tease out the values underlying activities such as dancing and sculpting. I wanted to help her see that, although she couldn't currently do those activities, she could still live the values that underpinned them.

So I asked, "If someone wanted to really get into sculpting—to enjoy it, appreciate it, do it well—what qualities do you think would help them to do that?"

"Errm, well—I guess dedication...trying new things...focus...persistence...creativity...striving to grow or improve...being real...allowing yourself to make mistakes and learn from them."

"And are those qualities important to you? Do they describe how you like to sculpt?"

"Yes! But I can't do it anymore!"

"Yes, and, of course, that's very painful."

At this point, Rada burst into tears, flooded with sadness and anger, so we dropped anchor and practiced the kind hands exercise. (As we do the painful work of rebuilding, we can expect emotional storms to keep blowing in, so it's important to keep using all the mindfulness and self-compassion skills we covered in part 1.) After the exercise, we returned to the discussion.

"What you've been describing there—persistence, creativity, dedication, focus, growth, and so on—sound like important values."

"Yes," said Rada. "They are."

"So, are these values only for that one activity, sculpting? Or are there other activities in your life—activities you can do today even with all the limitations imposed by your illness—where you could bring some of these values into play? Obviously, that wouldn't be the same as sculpting, and nor would it get rid of your pain. But I'm wondering, could there be something in it that's meaningful for you?"

Rada paused for a long time, thinking very carefully. Then, ever so slowly she nodded her head.

If you didn't actually do the "How's Your Mind Trying to Help?" exercise earlier in this chapter, or you zipped through it quickly without reflecting on the questions, please go back and take your time with it. See if you can dig out some values.

If your mind is like Rada's, pushing you to do something that's currently unrealistic or impossible, then identify the values that underpin that activity. A good way to do this is to ask yourself, *If someone wanted to enjoy, appreciate, or do this activity well, what personal qualities would help them to do so?*

You may recall I mentioned earlier that many people question themselves after a major loss: *Who am I? Who am I without my job? Who am I without a partner...my health...my parents...my child?* If your mind does this, then it's trying to help you think deeply about what sort of person you want to be, what values you want to live by, what you want to stand for in the face of your loss. Hopefully, the exercises in this chapter will help you to answer those questions.

Remember, our aim at this point is simply to get a sense of what our values are. In the next chapter, we'll look at how to translate them into actions (and you'll find out what Natalie and Rada did next). So, to get some more clarity about your values, here's another exercise called "Connect and Reflect." (This was inspired by a similar exercise called "The Sweet Spot," created by one of my mentors, Kelly Wilson.) I invite you to try it.

Connect and Reflect

Part 1: Connect

Begin this exercise by taking a few moments to drop anchor.

Now think of someone who is active *in your life today*—someone you care about, see regularly, and with whom you like to spend quality time. Remember a recent time when you were with each other, doing something you really like to do.

Make this memory as vivid as possible, as if it's happening here and now.

Relive it. Feel it emotionally.

Notice where you are and what it's like: Time of day? Indoors or outdoors? Weather? Scenery? Temperature? What's the air like? What can you see? What can you hear? What can you touch...taste...smell?

Notice the other person: What does she look like? What is he saying or doing? What's her tone of voice, the expression on his face, her body posture, the way he moves?

In this memory, what are you thinking? And feeling? And doing? What are you doing with your arms...legs...mouth? Are you moving or still? Get into your body (in this memory); what does it feel like?

See if you can tap into the emotion of this memory; what does it *feel* like? Drink it in and let it flow through you; open up and make room for it. You may well find as you do this, that you encounter some sadness, longing, or regret. This is hardly surprising, because whatever we hold precious will usually bring us pain. So, as you engage with this memory, be open and make room for all that arises: the pleasure *and* the pain.

Savor the moment. Make the most of it. Really appreciate it.

So how did you find that? Did you find it enjoyable? Did sadness or other painful emotions arise? If so, did you open up and make room for them, and practice self-compassion? That was actually just the first part of the exercise. The second part is to go back into that memory, take a good look at yourself—and reflect.

Part 2: Reflect

Now step back and look at the memory as if you're watching it on TV.

Focus on yourself. What are you saying and doing? How are you interacting with the other person? How are you treating him or her? How are you responding to him or her?

What qualities are you showing in this memory? For example, are you being open, engaged, interested, loving, kind, fun loving, playful, connected, appreciative, honest, real, courageous, intimate?

What does this remind you about the sort of person you want to be?

What does this tell you about the way you want to treat yourself and others?

What does this highlight about the sort of relationships you want to build, and how you want to spend your time?

I'm guessing that in the "Connect and Reflect" exercise you remembered a deep connection with someone. Now consider, in that memory, what are you bringing to the table? For example, are you contributing love, enthusiasm, curiosity, openness, attentiveness, appreciation, gratitude, sensuality, kindness, interest, playfulness, humor, warmth, affection, tenderness, honesty, trust?

Find three or four words that best describe the qualities of your behavior in that memory. Are those qualities you *want* to bring to life's table? Are those qualities you *want* to bring into your relationships through your words, gestures, deeds, and actions? If so, then these too are your values.

Okay, now let's do one last exercise.

Looking Back Six Months from Now

Begin this exercise by taking a few moments to drop anchor. Now imagine that six months from now you are looking back on your life today, thinking about how you responded to your loss. From that perspective, answer some or all of these questions. (Take your time—really think about each question.)

What did you stand for in the face of your loss?

How did you treat yourself as you went through it?

How did you treat the people you care about as you went through it?

As you dealt with all the difficulties, what qualities did you bring to life's table?

I hope you're getting a sense now of some of your values. Sometimes our minds make this process very hard for us: *How do I know if these are my real values? Am I just picking them because I think I should have these as my values?* and so on. When you notice your mind doing that, name it: *Ah, here's my mind overanalyzing, I'm having thoughts of self-doubt, I'm noticing double-guessing.* Instead of getting caught up in "analysis paralysis," pick a few values to play around with and notice what happens. When you start using these values in the manner that we discuss in the next chapter, you'll learn a lot about yourself—and usually it will rapidly become clear whether or not you've found your real values.

Values, Relationships, and Meaning

Let's think of our life as a huge, complex network of relationships. When I use the term "relationship," I mean the way we interact with anyone or anything. In this sense of the word, we have relationships with ourselves; our thoughts, feelings, and memories; our body; our family, friends, and neighbors; our work and leisure; our physical environment; and with a vast number of inanimate objects such as our phone, computer, food, water, bed, home, and so on.

Rebuilding our life involves looking at the relationships we have and doing what we can to make them as healthy as possible. Sometimes we might buy into unhelpful stories such as The Life-Has-No-Meaning Story, The I-Don't-Know-What-to-Do-with-My-Life Story, or The Is-This-All-There-Is? Story. But, at any moment, all we need to do to infuse our life with a sense of meaning and purpose is to choose a relationship that matters—with anyone or anything—and do something to make it better, healthier, or more fulfilling. How do we that? By noticing what life is serving up in this moment and bringing our values to the table.

For example, if somebody in your life is toxic, abusive, hurtful, uncaring, or heartless, you might choose to bring to the table qualities such as assertiveness, courage, fairness, self-respect, self-protection, self-support. Guided by these values, you protect and look after yourself and actively reduce or stop the damage done by the other person. (This could involve restricting contact with them or even cutting them out of your life altogether.) Similarly, if there's an activity in your life that is self-defeating (e.g., withdrawing from or fighting with your loved ones), or a substance you take that is toxic in excess (e.g., tobacco, alcohol, junk food), then you might choose to bring to the table qualities such as self-awareness and self-care to actively break that pattern.

If somebody in your life is warm and caring, then you might choose to bring qualities such as appreciation, gratitude, love, kindness, and trust. If there's an activity in your life that enriches or enhances it (such as connecting with your loved ones, having fun, listening to music, reading books, pursuing your hobbies or interests), then you might choose to bring qualities such as being attentive, focused, interested, open, curious, engaged, or appreciative.

Many self-help approaches focus on goals: on what we want to *get* from life and our relationships. Our values give rise to a very different attitude: they help us to look at what we want to actively *contribute* to life; what we want to *give* to our relationships. We'll look at goals later, because they are very important—we're not going to pretend we don't need or want anything in life. But for now, let's focus on values and consider what happens when we actively bring them to the table. For example, consider your relationship with this book. As you read, are you bringing in qualities of openness, enthusiasm, curiosity, focus, engagement? And does that make a difference? Have you ever had a relationship with a book where you *didn't* bring in qualities like these? If so, was it rewarding and fulfilling—or did it feel like a waste of time?

For another example, let's go back to the "Connect and Reflect" exercise. In that moment, you were contributing qualities that actively enhanced the relationship. How often do we contribute very different qualities—such as aggression, unkindness, unfairness, disinterest, or disengagement—to our relationships with the people we love the most? And what happens to a relationship when that's what we bring to the table?

For one final example, let's go back to part 1. What happens to our relationship with ourselves when we contribute qualities such as being harsh, unkind, judgmental, or uncaring? And what happens when we bring different qualities, such as kindness and caring?

The great thing about knowing our values is that we can *instantly* use them to make our life more meaningful. We don't have to wait until we find some noble cause or life mission; we can simply bring our values into any relationship—with anyone or anything—here and now. In the next chapter, we'll look at how to do that, but in the meantime let's finish with something to reflect on—a quote from the Canadian poet Henry Drummond: "You will find, as you look back upon your life, that the moments when you have really lived are the moments when you have done things in the spirit of love."

14 One Small Step

Have you heard this saying—"It's the thought that counts"?

Let's think about this. Which means more to you—when someone has a thought about buying you a birthday present, or when they actually go out and buy you one? Which of these will get you into trouble with the law—if you have thoughts about committing a crime, or if you actually go out and commit one? Which will count the most to your children—if you think about being a loving and supportive parent, or if you actually are loving and supportive?

So let's face it: it's our actions that count, not our thoughts. And it's just as well, or we'd all be in a lot of trouble. Think of all those angry, vengeful thoughts you've had in your life, of all those times you've thought of hurting another person, such as yelling insults, saying nasty put-downs, or committing acts of revenge. And have you ever had thoughts about leaving your partner, quitting your job, or running away from your life? We all have plenty of thoughts that we would be embarrassed to admit in public, so what state would our lives be in if these thoughts *really did* count more than our actions?

We create our life through our actions, not through our thoughts. A client of mine has been seriously thinking about quitting his dull, tedious, undemanding job and retraining as a psychologist. The problem? He's been thinking about it for over ten years—and he still hasn't taken any action! Isn't he a bit like you and me? Most of us spend too much time thinking about what we want to do on this planet, but not enough time actually doing it.

So, the next time you're *thinking* about an important or meaningful area of your life, ask yourself these questions: *What's a tiny step I could take? What's the smallest, easiest, simplest action I could do to make a difference in this part of my life?* After all, when it comes to creating the life you want, even the tiniest actions count more than hundreds of hours of thinking.

This is where our values can really help us. We can ask ourselves two simple questions:

- What relationship matters most in this moment?

- What do I want to bring to the table?

Suppose the relationship that matters most right now is with your body. Could you bring openness and curiosity to the table? Could you notice what your body is doing? How is it moving? Where is it tense—and relaxed? Where is it strong—and weak? What makes it function better—and worse? Could you bring in some kindness and caring for your body through stretching, exercise, eating well, sleeping well, resting, walking, or teaching it a new skill?

If the most important relationship is with your mind, could you bring openness and curiosity to the table? Notice what your mind is up to. Is it doing something useful? Is it fantasizing, remembering, worrying, pondering, or planning? If you wanted to be caring and helpful, could you give your mind a rest, could you teach it a new skill, or could you introduce it to something interesting like some new books, music, or movies?

If the most important relationship is with your art, sport, hobby, work, or study, what happens when you bring interest and attentiveness to the table? When you immerse your full attention in the task? When you give it your enthusiasm, curiosity, courage, creativity, care, consideration, or patience?

And if your most important relationship is with a person, then the same question applies, whoever that person is—your partner, child, parent, friend, neighbor, teacher, student, employer, coworker, or someone else. Do you want to be engaged, curious, attentive, open, caring—or disengaged, uninterested, inattentive, closed off, uncaring? If the former, there are ways you can instantly do this. You might pay more attention to their face, tone of voice, body posture, or the words they're saying. You might be curious about their emotions, thoughts, or their beliefs, attitudes, and assumptions. You might try to understand their world and their needs, or do small acts of kindness and caring.

Of course, if this other person treats you badly, you'll need to take care of and contribute to *your own* health and well-being by doing what's necessary to protect yourself and meet your own needs. And if the bad treatment persists, you may consider ending the relationship, if that's possible. Either way, while the relationship persists, your priority should be on caring for yourself within it.

In the last chapter, you connected with your values. The challenge now is to translate values into actions. What can you say—silently to yourself or out aloud to others—that brings your values to the table? What can you do with your arms and your legs, your hands and your feet, the expressions on your face, the postures of your body, the tone of your voice that puts your values into play?

One Brick at a Time

In chapter 13, we talked about how walls are built one brick at a time. It's wise to take this same step-by-step approach to rebuilding our life after loss so we don't get overwhelmed. With this in mind, think of your life in terms of four overarching domains:

- work and education
- family and friends
- play and leisure
- health and well-being

Each week, I recommend you pick *just one* of these four domains to actively work on.

The work and education domain includes paid work, volunteer work, or any area of study, training, or learning. Family and friends can include your children, parents, partner, relatives, friends, and anyone else you care deeply about. Play and leisure includes your hobbies, interests, creative pursuits, sports that you play or follow, and anything you like to do for rest or relaxation. Health and well-being includes anything you do to actively contribute to your life physically, emotionally, spiritually, or psychologically. (Of course, these domains overlap—they're not really separate at all. This is just a convenient way of looking at different aspects of your life. The good news is, because of the interconnectedness of these domains, there's often a domino effect: while you're working on one, it impacts positively on another.)

Once you've chosen a domain to work on, pick two or three values you want to bring to the table. (If you really want to, you can choose up to four or five values, but it's hard to remember more than that.) Then consider how you might actively live those values within that domain. What new activities might you start? How might you modify activities you're already doing? What actions might you take? What words might you say? How might you treat yourself, others, or the world around you?

Antonio chose to work first in the family and friends domain, with a special focus on his relationship with Cathy. And he chose the values of kindness, understanding, and openness. He stopped drinking heavily, zoning out in front of the TV, picking fights. He started listening to her with genuine kindness, holding her when she cried, and going for a long walk with her in the evenings when they would both talk openly and honestly about their grief. This didn't take away Antonio's grief and suffering, but it did give him a sense of being true to himself, of being the sort of partner he really wanted to be deep in his heart.

Shanti also chose the family and friends domain, and the values of courage, openness, and honesty. One by one, she started to reconnect with her friends and family; this was very courageous as it brought up huge feelings of shame and anxiety. She also chose to be honest and open about those feelings rather than hide them and put on a happy face. To her surprise, she found most of her loved ones were kind and understanding. Unfortunately, some of them were inept at providing the support she needed—and her mother, appallingly, blamed Shanti for the affair: "If you'd been a better wife, he wouldn't have gone looking." So Shanti also brought along her values of self-compassion and self-protection. She minimized time with her mother and treated herself kindly whenever her mother was toxic. Instead she spent most of her time with the people who could truly be there for her in a loving and nurturing way. This didn't get rid of her sadness, anger, or painful memories, but it did give her a sense of reclaiming her life.

Dave had lost his job, so not surprisingly the domain he chose first was work and education. The values he picked were patience, persistence, and responsibility. He allocated eight hours every day where he would either actively pursue the goal of finding a new job, or actively educate himself in skills and knowledge that would help him in that pursuit. The tedious tasks of writing a résumé, searching for jobs, applying for jobs, and going for interviews gave Dave ample opportunities to live his values. Each morning, as he prepared himself for all those unpleasant (and unpaid) tasks he needed to do, he'd drop anchor and repeat his values silently, like a mantra: *Patience, persistence, responsibility.* This didn't make his tasks easy or fun, but it did give him a sense of empowerment. He had no power to escape all the discomfort and hassle that's involved in finding a new job. He also had no power to ensure that he'd get the job he wanted. But he did have the power to choose his own attitude, to choose what he'd bring to the table in the face of his difficulties.

Natalie chose to focus on health and well-being. The values she picked were self-care and self-kindness. She practiced the kind hands exercise every day and worked hard at unhooking from The Bad Mother Story. She'd lost a lot of weight since Richard's death and was now unhealthily thin. So, even though she still had no appetite, in the service of self-care, she started drinking protein shakes to increase her caloric intake. Of course, this could never bring her son back or diminish her agony at his loss. But it did give her a sense of establishing a little control amid all the chaos. And it did help her to tap into those nurturing, caring instincts she'd always had as a mother.

Rada chose to focus on the domain of play and leisure, and to bring in the values of creativity, persistence, and openness—openness to trying new things as well as openness to making mistakes and learning from them. She couldn't sculpt or dance, but she found other ways to bring those values to the table. For example, she experimented with her stretching and strengthening exercises, and ways of doing them in time to very slow, rhythmic, soothing music—like an ultra-slow-motion minimalist dance routine. It was a long way from Latin dancing, but nonetheless it offered her a way to live her values of creativity, openness, and persistence (and make her physical therapy routine a lot more interesting). She also started a new creative activity, something that she hadn't done since high school: pencil drawing. It was nothing remotely like sculpting, and she had no "natural talent," as she put it, but it did give her the satisfaction of being creative and open to learning.

So now, let's come back to you. I encourage you, for at least the next month, to pick one domain each week to focus on. (It can be the same domain every week, if you like; you don't have to change, if you prefer not to.) And pick two or three values (five at most) to play with, and start actively bringing them in to what you do.

If you're not clear about what to do differently, then keep doing what you're doing—but now, as you do those activities, look for opportunities to "flavor" them with your values. For example, let's suppose you choose the domain of family and friends, and the values of warmth and playfulness. When you're with your loved ones, look for opportunities to sprinkle a bit of warmth and kindness into the interaction through the words you say or the things you do, or even through the expression on your face and your tone of voice.

And as you flavor the moment with those values, also take the time to savor it. Actively notice and appreciate the difference it makes. Notice what it's like to behave the way you really want to, deep in your heart. What's it like for you? What's it like for the people you care about? Is life more meaningful, more fulfilling? Is this something you would like to do more often? Flavor your moments with values and savor what happens when you do so.

Flavoring and Savoring

Whether you start doing new things—like Rada with her drawing and Dave with his job search—or you keep on doing much the same as before, liberally sprinkle your values into your life. One way to do this is with a simple drill that takes less than a minute. Once or twice a day, take a few moments to drop anchor, and think of two or three values that you want to bring to the table in the next few hours. (It may be the same two or three values every time, or you may prefer to change them.) Then as you go through the day, look for opportunities to flavor your activities with those values.

Be flexible with this. You can sprinkle your values into other domains as well; you don't have to stick to the one you've chosen to focus on. Likewise, if there's an opportunity to sprinkle in some different values (i.e., different than the ones you chose in the morning), then please, don't hold back. Flavor your experiences with your values, and savor what happens when you do so.

15   The Challenge Formula

Life is both kind and cruel; it doles out both wonder and dread in generous servings. In my years as a general practitioner, I met many people who had suffered terribly in life. I saw children disfigured by fire and babies with fatal diseases, strong capable adults reduced to invalids and brilliant minds wiped away by dementia, and bodies misshapen and deformed through all manner of injury—the victims of violence and disaster. I saw refugees from foreign lands, struggling to rebuild their lives after rape and torture, or to start again after losing most of their family. I saw the freshly bereaved, howling in their anguish; distraught mothers clutching their stillborn babies. I saw men with weeping sores and blistering skin, and women with broken bones and bleeding arteries. I saw the blind, the deaf, and the paralyzed, the seriously ill, and the newly deceased.

And in the midst of all this pain, I saw courage, kindness, and compassion. I saw people reaching out and helping each other, families bonding through crisis, friends and neighbors holding each other's hands. I saw men and women facing death with dignity and love and affection pouring from broken hearts. I saw parents slowly rebuilding shattered lives and finding the strength within to persist and grow.

A terrible crisis can prompt us to open our hearts and search within—to reach inside and discover what we are made of. However, this may take a while—and our capacity to do this may vary from hour to hour, day to day, week to week. There'll likely be times when we want to give up on life—and we do that, times when it's all too much, and we just want to retreat.

This, as I've said before, is natural. We try to escape using different methods—anything from movies and music to drinking and drugs. Even if our escape is only momentary, the relief is huge. However, a life lived in retreat is not fulfilling, and fighting our thoughts and feelings is exhausting. As the Indian poet Rabindranath Tagore put it, "You can't cross the sea merely by standing and staring at the water." So if we want to thrive in the face of loss, our best option is to open ourselves to life as it is in this moment and to stand for something that matters deep in our heart.

The Challenge Formula

To help us thrive in the face of loss, I'd like to share a new strategy with you—the challenge formula, which is spelled out in the options below. But before we get into the specifics of it, please remember that no matter how great the challenge we face, we are not powerless. We have choices. Even in the most difficult situations, we always have either two or three options:

Option 1. Leave.

Option 2. Stay and live by your values: do whatever you can to improve the situation, make room for the inevitable pain that goes with it, and hold yourself kindly.

Option 3. Stay and do things that either make no difference or make it worse.

Option 1—leave—isn't always available. For example, if you're in prison or a refugee camp, you can't just leave. If you've got a serious illness or you've lost a loved one, you can't simply leave that situation; wherever you go, the problem goes with you. But at times, leaving the situation *is* an option—in which case, seriously consider it. For example, if you're in a toxic relationship, an awful job, a violent neighborhood, consider this: is your life likely to be richer, fuller, more meaningful if you leave that situation rather than stay?

Now if you can't leave, won't leave, or don't consider leaving to be the best option, then you are down to options 2 and 3. Unfortunately, for most of us, option 3 comes quite naturally: *Stay and do things that either make no difference or make it worse.* In challenging situations, we get hooked by difficult thoughts and feelings, and pulled into self-defeating patterns of behavior that either keep us stuck or make things worse. We may turn to excessive use of drugs and alcohol, fighting with or withdrawing from loved ones, dropping out of important parts of life, or many other self-defeating behaviors. (I've often fallen into these patterns, and I'm pretty sure you have too.)

So the path to a better life clearly lies in option 2: *Stay and live by your values, and do whatever you can to improve the situation.* And, of course, you can't expect to feel happy when you're in a really difficult situation; you will have many painful thoughts and feelings. So the second part of option 2— *make room for the inevitable pain and hold yourself kindly*—is very relevant. That's why we spent so much time earlier learning how to make room for painful thoughts, feelings, and memories, how to lessen their impact, how to allow them to be present without jerking us around, and how to respond to our pain with genuine kindness.

The life of Nelson Mandela gives an excellent example of the challenge formula in action. For twenty-seven years, he was imprisoned by the South African government. Why? Because he dared to fight for freedom and democracy and to oppose apartheid, the official government policy of racial discrimination. Now option 1 of the formula was clearly out: he couldn't *leave* prison. So mostly, he chose option 2. He made room for his painful feelings, and he lived according to his values: standing for freedom, equality, and peace. For instance, during his first seventeen years in prison on Robben Island, Mandela had to do hard labor in a lime quarry. But he turned the situation to his advantage. Mandela knew that education was essential for equality and democracy, so he arranged illegal meetings in the tunnels of the quarry where the prisoners would teach and instruct each other. (Later this came to be known as "Mandela University.")

One of the most remarkable aspects of Mandela's story is that in 1985, after twenty-two years in prison, the South African government offered to release him, but he turned them down! Why? Because the condition for release was that he would have to remain silent, that he would refrain from speaking out against apartheid. For Mandela to do this, he would have had to go against his core values, so he chose to stay in prison instead. That meant *another five years in prison* before he was finally released without this condition! And yet, despite this huge blow, he was able to find fulfillment in standing for something: freedom, democracy, and equality. Mandela's case is extraordinary, but the challenge formula applies to every one of us, no matter what our situation is. If we can't or won't leave, then we can stay and live by our values, do what we can to improve things, and make room for the pain that's inevitable.

In chapter 1, I mentioned an ACT program that I wrote for the World Health Organization for use in refugee camps around the world. The program consists mostly of audio recordings; the refugees, in small groups, listen to them. The recordings explain ACT concepts and then ask the group members to do exercises similar to the ones in this book. The challenge formula comes in early, in the very first session. The reality is, if you're in a refugee camp, you can't just leave , so option 1 is out. But you still have choices between options 2 and 3. For example, you share your tent with others, and you can treat them with kindness, warmth, and openness—or you can treat them with aggression, coldness, or hostility. And the choices you make will alter your experience within that tent. And when you leave the tent, the same holds true. You can be kind and friendly to your neighbors in other tents, or distant and unfriendly. You can join community activities such as singing or prayer, or you can isolate yourself from them.

The more you choose option 2—*Stay and live by your values: do whatever you can to improve the situation, make room for the inevitable pain that goes with it, and hold yourself kindly*—the better your quality of life within the camp.

Being Realistic

When it comes to option 2, it's important to be realistic. If you're in prison or in a refugee camp, or suffering from a serious illness or injury, there are many things you can't do. But focusing on what you *can't* do is a recipe for misery. It's much wiser to focus on what you *can* do. Remember Rada? Her mind kept pushing her to sculpt and dance when it wasn't realistic to do those things, and that depressed her. But when she focused on what she *could* do, living her values in other ways, her life was far more fulfilling.

So far I've focused mainly on small steps, actions, and behavior changes. When we rebuild our lives after a loss, we do it mostly through these small changes. If we set big goals, they may backfire because we often don't have the time, energy, or other resources to achieve these goals. We become overwhelmed and give up. Small changes are much easier to make and sustain, and over time they often have dramatic effects. Sometimes, however, we do need to set goals for ourselves, and, if so, it's important to make them realistic. Effectively setting goals is a skill that most of us are not naturally good at. So, if you'd like some help, see appendix C, which will guide you step by step through the process. And once you've set some goals, the next step is to take action!

We can never know in advance if we'll achieve our goals or not, but we *can* take action right away. When we do, we will experience a sense of empowerment, a sense of embracing life and making the most of it, instead of letting it pass us by.

Willingness

When I present the challenge formula to my clients, most feel empowered: it helps them to realize they have choices. However, occasionally, someone reacts strongly and negatively, usually with a mixture of anger and anxiety. Why? Usually they find it too confronting. The challenge formula confronts us with the reality that we have choices, and therefore we are responsible for how we act. Option 3 offers short-term relief as we buy the story that there's nothing we can do, so we may as well give up and stop trying. This relieves us of responsibility. But any such relief does not last long. In the long run, this option drains the life from us. Our vitality lies only in taking a stand: in choosing options 1 or 2. However, we will only experience this vitality if we take our stand with a quality known as "willingness."

What does *willingness* mean? Psychologist Hank Robb explains it like this: Suppose you hand over $20 for a movie ticket. You can give the money resentfully or grudgingly, or you can give the money willingly, but either way you have to hand over the money. When you pay willingly, the experience is far more fulfilling than if you do so resentfully.

So when we take a stand, let's do so willingly. If we take this stand hooked by *I have no choice, I hate having to do this, I shouldn't have to do this, This is my lot in life,* or *I have to do it; it's my duty,* we will feel burdened, disempowered, or drained. There is no "have to," "must," "ought," or "should" in a value. Such words only turn our values into life-draining rules.

How do we distinguish rules from values? Well, "rules" can usually be identified by words or phrases like these:

- right/wrong
- good/bad
- should/shouldn't
- have to/must/ought
- can't unless…
- shouldn't because…
- won't until…

Rules tell you how to live your life: the right and wrong way of doing things. Values do *not* do this; values simply describe the qualities you wish to bring to your ongoing behavior. So "Thou shalt not kill" is a rule. It tells you what you should and shouldn't do; what is right and wrong. The values underneath this rule are caring and respect for human life. If being loving is your value, this is obviously very different from a rule such as "You *must* always be loving, no matter what!" If being kind is your value, that's a world apart from a rule like "You *should* be kind at all times, even when people are abusive to you." If being efficient is your value, that's a long way from the rule that "You *must* do it perfectly or there's no point."

Of course, we can use our values to help set rules that guide us, but we do need to be clear that they are not the same thing. Values give us a sense of freedom because there are so many different ways in which we can act on them. In contrast, rules often give us a sense of restriction or obligation; they often weigh us down and limit our options. Suppose we help someone out because we're consciously in touch with our values: we wish to be kind and generous. Now compare this to helping someone out because we're hooked by rules: "it's the right thing to do," we "should do it," we "owe them," or we "are obliged to." The values approach tends to be freeing and energizing; the rules approach is often restrictive, draining, and burdensome.

So if you feel drained, burdened, or resentful as you take a stand, pause for a moment, and notice what unhelpful story has hooked you. Then name the story and drop anchor to help yourself unhook. After this, come back to your values and recognize that you *do* have a choice. You can *choose* to stand for something—or not. You certainly don't *have to.* The big questions to ask yourself are these: *Am I willing to take a stand in the face of this loss? Am I willing to make room for my pain and act on my values?*

16   The Prison of Resentment

Do you ever get caught up in resentment? Many of us do, especially after a major loss. We may resent others because they let us down, treated us badly, didn't care about us, achieved more than us, are better off than us, or for dozens of other reasons. Resentment is a particularly sticky version of The Not Good Enough Story, heavily infused with anger, self-righteousness, and a strong sense of injustice.

When resentment hooks us, it almost always pulls us into self-defeating struggles. In Buddhism, they say, "Resentment is like grasping a red-hot coal in order to throw it at someone else." In Alcoholics Anonymous (AA), they say, "Resentment is like swallowing poison and hoping the other person dies." These sayings share the idea that when we get hooked by resentment, all we do is hurt ourselves even more than we already have been.

Resentment comes from the French word *resentir*, which means "to feel again." Each time resentment hooks us we *feel again* our hurt, anger, and sense of unfairness or injustice. The events happened in the past, but as we dwell on them in the present, we *feel again* all that pain. And, as we stew in our anger and dissatisfaction, our vitality seeps away.

Self-blame—resentment turned on ourselves—is similar. Again and again our minds remind us of what we did wrong, then we get angry and judge or punish ourselves. We *feel again* all our pain, regret, angst, disappointment, and anxiety. This does not alter the past nor does it enable us to learn and grow from our mistakes; all we achieve is hurting ourselves more. Although we know this logically and rationally, we still keep doing it.

Forgiveness

So what is the antidote to resentment and self-blame? It is "forgiveness"—but not forgiveness as we commonly think of it. In the ACT model, forgiveness does *not* mean forgetting, nor does it mean that what happened was okay, excusable, or unimportant, nor does it involve saying or doing anything to someone else.

To understand the ACT notion of forgiveness, consider the origin of the word. "Forgive" is derived from two separate words: "give" and "before." So in ACT, forgiveness simply means *giving* yourself back what life was like *before* resentment took over. At some point in the past, something very painful happened. Either *you* did something that you now blame yourself for, or *others* did something that you now blame them for. Since then, your mind has repeatedly pulled you back to those events so you feel the pain again and again, along with the blaming, judging, and struggling.

What was your life like *before* resentment took over? Were you getting on with life and making the most of it? Were you living in the present? Even if your life *wasn't* very good before resentment took over, at least you weren't lost in the smog of resentment and self-blame. So how about giving back to yourself the clarity and freedom of life without all that smog? In ACT, forgiveness is something you do purely for yourself. It's *giving* yourself a life free from the burden of resentment or self-blame.

How do we cultivate this type of forgiveness? When our minds generate stories that feed resentment or self-blame, we notice and name them, saying something like *I'm noticing my mind beating me up, I'm having a painful memory, Here's my mind judging me,* or *I'm having thoughts about being bad.* We also hold ourselves kindly. No matter where we place the blame—on ourselves or on others—we are hurting. So let's be kind, compassionate, hold ourselves gently, make room for our feelings, and get present.

We will often need to drop anchor repeatedly to engage again in the present. When present, we can act from our values, infusing our actions with purpose. We can then take a stand in the face of our loss.

For example, if we genuinely did something "wrong," "bad," or "careless"—and it's not just the mind being overly critical—then we could now take a stand to make amends. Michael, an alcoholic and Vietnam veteran, told me this was impossible for him: he'd killed several people in the war and there was no way to make amends for that. It was hard to argue with that, so I didn't even try. Instead I said, "Beating yourself up and drinking yourself into the grave doesn't alter the past. And yes, of course, you can't make amends to the dead; you can't do *anything* for them. But you *can* do something now that can contribute in meaningful ways to the *living*. If you waste your life, then nothing good has come from those horrors of the past. But if you use your life to contribute to others, to make a difference in the world, then something good *has* come out of those horrors."

For Michael, this was a revelation. With a lot of hard work, eventually he was able to unhook himself from those self-blaming stories and treat himself kindly. Over the space of nine months, he joined an AA group, quit drinking, and started volunteering for two charitable organizations: one for the homeless and the other for refugees. This wasn't easy for him. It took a huge amount of effort, and he had to make room for enormous amounts of pain, but it paid off handsomely. Although he couldn't change the past, he found he could make a useful difference in the present—and as he did so, his life became far more fulfilling.

While most of us get entangled in self-blame at times, our stories are probably not as dramatic as Michael's; after all, most of us have never killed someone. However, that doesn't lessen the burden of our stories. The key thing is to practice being kind to yourself (even if your mind says you don't deserve it), saying such things as *I'm a fallible human being. Like every other person on the planet, I make mistakes, I screw things up, and I get things wrong. This is part of being human.* Then place a compassionate hand on your body, breathe into the pain, and acknowledge that it hurts. Remind yourself that self-punishment achieves nothing useful; vitality lies only in taking a stand. If there is something you can do to make amends, repair the damage, or turn the situation around, then it makes sense to do it. If there's nothing you *can* do along those lines (or if you're not yet *willing* to do it), then you can invest your energy in building the relationships you have by connecting, caring, and contributing. To do this is an act of self-forgiveness.

But what if someone else did the "bad stuff"? Well, we could respond in many different ways, depending on the specifics of the situation and the outcomes we are looking for. We might choose to take decisive action to ensure, as best we can, that something like this doesn't happen again: to take that person to court, lodge a complaint against them, or cut off all contact with them. Or we might choose to learn new skills that equip us better for dealing with such people in the future; this could include anything from self-defense classes to assertiveness and communication skills to attending a course on dealing with difficult people. Or we might join organizations, sign petitions, go on marches, raise funds, support causes to change laws, improve society, or make the world a better place. Or we might choose simply to put it behind us and focus on rebuilding our life, here and now.

Forgiveness, then, consists of these four steps: (1) drop anchor, (2) unhook from the story, (3) hold yourself kindly, and (4) take a stand. And the beautiful thing is…it's never too late to do this.

17 It's Never Too Late

I never would have believed it possible—not in a million years. My dad was a fairly typical guy for his generation. He looked after his kids in the traditional ways: he worked hard to pay the bills and ensured that his six children all had food and clothes, a roof over their head, and a good education. He was very kind and loving in his own way. And like most men of his generation (and many men of my own), he was terrified of intimacy. And by intimacy, I don't mean having sex; I mean emotional and psychological intimacy.

To be emotionally and psychologically intimate with another human requires two things:

- You need to open up and be real, "let the other person in," and share your true thoughts and feelings instead of hiding them away.

- You need to create a space for the other person to do likewise—to be warm, open, and accepting enough that they too can be real and open with you.

My dad never talked about anything deeply personal. He liked to exchange facts, figures, and ideas; to discuss movies, books, and science. Although we had plenty of enjoyable conversations, I never got to know him very well. I never got to know about the feelings he struggled with, his hopes and dreams, his setbacks and failures, his most important life experiences and what he learned from them. I never got to know what made him frightened, angry, insecure, sad, or guilty. I knew virtually nothing of his interior world.

At seventy-eight, he developed lung cancer, but he didn't tell me. Not knowing his diagnosis, I went on a six-week trip overseas. Before I left, my dad had a full head of thick white hair, but when I returned he was totally bald. He didn't tell me that was due to chemotherapy. Instead, he told me he'd shaved off his hair because it was fashionable and thought it made him look younger. And I believed him.

As he got sicker and frailer, the true story emerged. But even then, he didn't want to talk about his cancer, the treatment, or his fears. Whenever I tried to talk about it, he changed the subject or got quiet.

Not knowing how long he'd live, I tried to tell him what he meant to me: how much I loved him, the role he'd played in my life, how he'd inspired me, the most useful things he'd taught me, and my fondest memories of him. Uncomfortable with such conversations, especially when my eyes brimmed with tears, he'd end them almost as soon as they started.

Miraculously, he recovered. I hoped this brush with death would help him to open up a little, but I was disappointed. He remained as closed as he'd always been, if not more so.

Three years later, at eighty-one, he had a heart attack. Major blockages in several coronary arteries required open-heart surgery, which carried significant risk. Talking to him shortly before surgery, I tried again to share with him what he meant to me as a father. Tears welled up in my eyes— tears of love and sadness—and he instantly closed off. He turned away and said, in a stern voice, "Hush now. And wipe away those tears."

Dad survived the operation, but afterward he had one complication after another and spent nearly a year in the hospital. Toward the end of that year, he became increasingly weak and demoralized. But he still wouldn't allow me to talk to him on an intimate level. Eventually, he decided he'd had enough of life and stopped all his medication. Being a doctor himself, he knew what this meant: effectively he was killing himself. Once medication ceased, he knew he'd have only a few days to live. Even knowing this, he still refused to let me tell him how much I loved him and what he meant to me.

As he neared death, Dad started hallucinating. But in between the hallucinations, he had lucid periods, where for several minutes at a time he'd be fully conscious and mentally alert. During one of these periods, I tried one last time to tell him what he meant to me and how much I loved him. I was a blubbering mess, tears streaming down my face and snot bubbling out of my nose. To my utter amazement, Dad turned and looked deep into my eyes. His face lit up with a radiant smile, full of kindness and compassion, and he took my hands in his and listened intently to everything I had to say, never once turning away or interrupting.

After I had finished sobbing and telling him everything I'd wanted to tell him for years, he said, in a voice full of tenderness and love, "Thank you." And then he added, "I love you too."

I tell this story to make two key points, both of them vital to cover before we end this section. The first is that small changes can have a profound impact. My dad did not transform his personality. All he did was make one small change: he made the effort to stay present and open. Even though our talk ended within minutes, that one small change gave rise to a beautiful and loving experience that I'll remember fondly until I die.

Our society bombards us with the notion that to have a better life, we have to dramatically overhaul all of it, radically transform our personality, or fundamentally alter the way we think—or all three! But when we buy into this notion, it doesn't usually help us; instead, we simply end up placing enormous pressure on ourselves. We push ourselves to be different and "better"—and we beat ourselves up for not meeting those expectations. Sadly, rather than raising us up, this just brings us down.

So why not lighten the load? Why not take the pressure off ourselves? Rome wasn't built in a day, and neither was a rich and meaningful life. Why not relax a little? Take baby steps. Go slow. And remember the moral of Aesop's much-loved tale *The Crow and the Pitcher*: "Little by little does the trick."

Trying to make huge changes in a short space of time is almost always a recipe for failure. Occasionally, we might manage it, but far more commonly we don't. However, small changes, over time, can make an enormous difference. As Archbishop Desmond Tutu said, "Do your little bit of good where you are; it's those little bits of good put together that overwhelm the world."

The second important point of this story is that it's never too late to make these little changes. Of course, our mind may not agree with that since it's a bit like a "reason-giving machine": it's brilliant at coming up with all sorts of reasons why we can't change, shouldn't change, or shouldn't have to change. One of its favorites is this: *It's too late! I can't change now. That's the way I am. That's the way I've always been.* But we don't have to buy into such thoughts. Instead of seeing ourselves as "carved in stone," we can acknowledge that we have a never-ending capacity to learn and grow, to act and think differently. All we need to do is tune into our hearts and ask ourselves, *What's one tiny change I could make? What's one tiny thing I could say or do differently that's more in line with the person I want to be?*

I wish my dad had made his change a bit earlier, instead of waiting until he was on his deathbed. But I am so grateful for his precious parting gift: he opened up, stayed present, and allowed me to share my true feelings with him. And he did this *willingly*. It is such a beautiful memory: both heart-warming and heart-rending at the same time. And it's a powerful reminder that as long as we're still breathing, it's never too late to do something meaningful.

18   Breaking Bad Habits

Mark Twain once said, "To cease smoking is the easiest thing in the world. I know because I've done it a thousand times." Even if we've never smoked, most of us can relate to Twain's witty observation. How often have you said, "I'll never do that again!' and the next day, you do it again? Or "Next time, I'm going to handle this differently! And next time you end up doing the same old thing!

Even when life's going well, it's easy to fall into "bad habits." But when we're coping with a big loss, our tendency to do so is much greater. By "bad habits," I mean the patterns of behavior that constitute option 3 of the challenge formula: *Stay and do things that either make no difference or make it worse.* This can include anything from excessive use of drugs and alcohol to withdrawal from friends and family, from aggression and conflict to avoiding important tasks or physical exercise.

We all have bad habits, and it would be foolhardy to try to break all of them. As I've said before, success comes by making small changes: lay one brick at a time. If you try to work on several bad habits at once, you're likely to get overwhelmed and give up. However, if there's *one* bad habit that's really important to work on, the good news is you now have all the skills you need to break it if you also put in the necessary time, effort, and commitment. To quote Mark Twain again: "Habit is habit, and not to be flung out of the window by any man, but coaxed downstairs a step at a time." If it's important to you, you *can* do it.

Changing Patterns of Behavior

There are six questions to answer when changing a self-defeating pattern of behavior:

1. What am I doing?

2. What triggers it?

3. What are the payoffs?

4. What are the costs?

5. What's the alternative?

6. What skills can I use?

Let's explore these one at a time.

1. What Am I Doing?

The first step in changing a problematic pattern of behavior is to specify what it involves: what are you actually saying and doing? For example, the term "procrastinating" doesn't specify what you *are* doing; it refers to what you're *not* doing. If you're procrastinating on some important task or activity, then specify what you are doing instead: are you playing computer games, reading the news, staring at the wall, eating snacks, petting the dog, lying in bed?

If the habit is "avoiding friends," what are you saying and doing? Are you ignoring text messages, declining invitations, making excuses, canceling social events at the last minute?

Antonio initially said that his problematic behavior was "drinking too much." I asked him to be more specific: "How much are you drinking?" He responded, "Seven or eight bottles of beer a night."

2. What Triggers It?

It's important to identify what triggers the behavior in question: what situations, thoughts, and feelings set it off? When and where does it happen? Do particular people, places, situations, events trigger it? What thoughts, feelings, memories, emotions, sensations, or urges show up immediately before you start doing it? (If you're not sure what thoughts and feelings trigger your behavior, keep a diary. Write down when and where you do it and see if you can identify what you were feeling and thinking just before you started.)

Antonio identified the triggering situation as returning home after work. His triggering thoughts and feelings were anxiety, guilt, tightness in his chest, knots in his stomach, painful memories of Sophia, thoughts like *Oh no. Here we go again—another tense evening*—and the urge to drink beer.

3. What Are the Payoffs?

Any type of behavior has both *payoffs* (outcomes that convey some sort of benefit) and *costs* (outcomes that are in some way detrimental). It's often helpful to identify what the payoffs are. Why? Because it gives insight into why you keep doing it. If there were no payoffs, you'd stop doing the behavior, so it's good to know what you're getting out of it. Basically, the payoffs boil down to this:

- you get away from something you don't want

- you get access to something you do want

Here are some of the most common payoffs for bad habits:

- We escape or avoid people, places, situations, or events that we find challenging.

- We escape or avoid unwanted thoughts, feelings, memories, sensations, or urges.

- We feel better.

- We get our needs met.

- We gain attention.

- We look good (to others or ourselves).

- We feel like we are right (and others are wrong).

- We feel like we are successfully following important rules.

- We feel like we're working hard on our problems.

- We feel like we're making sense of life, the world, ourselves, others, and so on.

Antonio could see that drinking helped him to (a) escape difficult thoughts and feelings, and (b) make him feel more relaxed. If you can't figure out the payoffs of your behavior, that's okay. You don't need to know them in order to change it; it's useful, but not essential.

4. What Are the Costs?

Presumably, you're already aware of some costs to this behavior or you wouldn't want to change it. However, it's worth reflecting more deeply on this issue. What does this behavior cost you in terms of health, well-being, vitality, relationships, money, wasted time, missed opportunities? What meaningful or valuable things do you lose or miss out on when you do this? What do you get that you don't want? (Don't beat yourself up. If your mind whacks you with that big stick and recites The Not Good Enough Story, drop anchor, unhook, and hold yourself kindly.)

Antonio knew the health costs of excessive alcohol use and also the negative impact on his marriage. But as he reflected more deeply, he recognized further costs: he slept poorly on nights when he drank heavily, which meant he woke up feeling sluggish, and was less focused and grumpier at work. On top of that, it pulled him away from his core values of being loving and supportive as a partner, which in turn triggered guilt and anxiety.

5. What's the Alternative?

It's easy to say, "I don't want to do XYZ anymore"; it's much harder to say, "Instead, I want to do ABC." However, this is an essential step in breaking the habit. When those triggers are present—all those difficult situations, thoughts, and feelings that you identified with question 2—and you're *not* going to do the behavior you identified in question 1, what will you do instead? This is where you come back to your values: what values-based actions will you take?

Antonio identified that instead of drinking heavily, he wanted to drink moderately: two bottles of beer a night instead of eight. So his new behavior was to drink those two beers slowly, stretching them out over two hours—and then to drink herbal tea or water for the rest of the evening.

6. What Skills Can I Use?

The information we gathered in answering questions 1 to 5 is useful, but the real change happens with question 6 when we actively apply our ACT skills. What skills can you use to handle all those triggering thoughts, feelings, memories, sensations, and urges—dropping anchor, unhooking from thoughts, making room for feelings, self-compassion, connecting with your values? Antonio used all of those skills to help him. As he drove home after work, he reminded himself of his values as a partner: being loving, caring, supportive, patient, understanding. When he got home, he waited three minutes before leaving his car. During that time, he dropped anchor, unhooked from his thoughts, and ran through his values again; then he opened up and made room for his feelings (including the urge to drink) and practiced self-compassion. Throughout the evening, he used these skills as often as he needed to. And as he flavored his evenings with the values of self-care, and being loving and supportive by drinking sensibly and spending quality time with his wife, he actively savored the difference this made in his life.

Did Antonio make these changes overnight? Did he do them perfectly? Did he stick to them ceaselessly? No, no, and no. He most certainly did not. Why not? Because Antonio, like the rest of us, is human. We are all flawed and fallible. We easily screw things up and let ourselves down. When that happens, it's painful, which is why we all need a lot more self-compassion.

Changing bad habits takes time, effort, and energy, and it's rarely a smooth process. Sometimes as we use our ACT skills, they'll work well— and other times they won't. Sometimes we'll forget to use them, or can't be bothered using them, or don't want to use them because, hey—we're human. So we can expect ups and downs, breakthroughs and setbacks, good patches and bad ones. That's the nature of changing our behavior.

It may take a long time before our new patterns become habitual— perhaps many months. For example, in my teens and twenties, I was an extremely heavy drinker—whereas these days, I hardly drink at all. So drinking excessively was a habit I successfully broke. But "unhealthy eating"—with a particular preference for chocolate, cake, and ice cream— is a habit I still struggle with intermittently. I go through periods where I successfully apply everything in this book and manage to eat pretty healthily. But I also go through phases where I stop applying ACT to this issue, and I fall back into unhealthy eating patterns, and stack on the weight. In other words, some habits are easier to break than others.

Maintaining New Habits

It's one thing to start some new life-enhancing behavior; it's another thing to keep it going. How can we sustain new patterns until they really become new habits? Well, we have lots of tools to help us with this challenge, but we can bundle them all into what I call "The Seven Rs": reminders, records, rewards, routines, relationships, reflecting, and restructuring. Let's take a look at each.

Reminders

We can create all sorts of simple tools to remind us of our new behavior. For example, we might create a pop-up or a screensaver on our computer or smartphone with an important word, phrase, or symbol that reminds us to act mindfully or to utilize a particular value. We can write a message on a card and stick it on the fridge, the bathroom mirror, or car dashboard. Or we might write something in a diary, calendar, or "notes" app of a smartphone—perhaps just one word like "breathe," "pause," or "patience," or a phrase like "'letting go" or "caring and compassionate." Alternatively, we might put a brightly colored sticker on the strap of our wristwatch, the back of our smartphone, or the keyboard of our computer, so that every time we see the sticker, it reminds us to do the new behavior.

Records

We can keep a record of our behavior throughout the day, noting when and where we do the new behavior and what the benefits are—and also when and where we do the old behavior and what the costs are. Any diary or notebook—on paper or on a computer screen—can serve this purpose.

Rewards

When we do a new behavior that involves acting on our values, hopefully that will be rewarding in itself. However, we can reinforce the new behavior with additional rewards. One form of reward is kind, encouraging self-talk—for example, saying to yourself, *Well done. I did it!* Another form is sharing your progress with a loved one who will respond positively. But you might prefer more material rewards. For example, if you sustain this new behavior for a week, you might buy or do something that you really like, such as getting a massage or buying a book.

Routines

If you get up every morning at the same time to exercise or do yoga, eventually that regular routine starts to come naturally and requires less willpower. So, try to build a routine or ritual around your new behavior so it becomes a regular part of your life. For example, if you drive home from work, then every night before you get out of your car, you might do two minutes of dropping anchor and reflect on what values you want to live by that evening.

Relationships

Whether you're studying or exercising, it's easier to do it if you have a "buddy." In AA programs, they team you up with a sponsor who helps you stay sober when the going gets tough. Can you find a kind, caring, encouraging person to support you with your new behavior? Maybe you can check in with this person regularly to share how well you're doing, or email him those records you've been keeping, or ask her to remind you to do the new behavior. For example, you might say, "When I raise my voice, can you please remind me to drop anchor?"

Reflecting

Regularly reflect on your behavior and how it affects your life. You can reflect in writing (records) or by talking with someone (relationships). Or you can do this as a mental exercise throughout the day, just before bed, or when you wake up in the morning. Take a few moments to reflect on questions like these:

- How am I doing?

- What am I doing that's working?

- What am I doing that's not working?

- What can I do more—or less—of, or do differently?

Make sure you also reflect on the times when you fall back into the old habit. Notice what triggers those relapses and setbacks, and notice what it costs you — that is, how do you suffer when that happens? Again, don't beat yourself up, but do reflect nonjudgmentally on the genuine costs to your health and well-being—and use this awareness to motivate yourself to get back on track.

Restructuring

We can often restructure our environment to make our new behavior easier and increase the chances we'll sustain it. For example, if the new behavior is "healthy eating," we can restructure the kitchen: get rid of or hide junk food, and stock the fridge and pantry with healthy stuff. If we want to go to the gym in the morning, we could pack up our sports gear and place it somewhere obvious and convenient so it's ready to go when we get up. (Our gym bag also acts as a reminder.)

So there you have it, "The Seven Rs." Now mix and match these methods to your heart's content and create your own set of tools for lasting change. Good luck!

Falling Back into Old Habits

Whoever said "practice makes perfect" was deluded. There's no such thing as perfection. Practice will help you establish better life skills, but it won't permanently eliminate self-defeating behaviors. You (and I, and everyone else on this planet) will screw up, make mistakes, and, at times, fall back into old habits. This will happen repeatedly. Indeed, because we humans screw up so often, I like to ask my clients two questions:

- The next time you screw up, what would you ideally say or do to handle it more effectively?

- If you've hurt yourself or others, what could you do to make amends and repair the damage?

Before answering these questions, reflect on your values and the sort of person you want to be. If you could respond mindfully, acting on your core values, then what would you say and do when you notice you've screwed up? Are you willing to forgive yourself, let go, and move on? Are you willing to make room for your painful feelings, unhook from unhelpful thoughts, be kind to yourself, and deal with the issue constructively instead of getting bogged down in self-recrimination?

Note that this doesn't mean we're giving up. It just means we're being realistic. With practice, we get much better at living by our values, engaging fully in life, practicing forgiveness and self-compassion, unhooking from difficult thoughts, and making room for difficult feelings. The more we practice, the better the outlook for our future. At the same time, we need to unhook from unrealistic expectations, to let go of trying to be perfect. The fact is, we will *not* always do what's most effective. We will *not* turn into saints or superheroes. We are human, which means we can never be perfect. No matter how well we apply the principles of ACT, and no matter how much they become "second nature," at times we will forget and fall back into old ways.

That's why, when I counsel clients, I always discuss the issue of "relapse." I might say, "Okay, you just made a commitment that, from now on, instead of yelling at your partner or your kids, you'll explain calmly and patiently why you're annoyed. Now I'm sure you're 100 percent sincere about that; you certainly seem genuinely determined to work on this. But let me ask, how likely is it that you will never, ever yell at your loved ones again?" In saying this, I'm not aiming to undermine their commitment; I'm simply introducing some realism. I've found that most people appreciate this honesty. It helps them to loosen their grip on The Do It Perfectly Story.

The bottom line is this: making changes is hard. We're all capable of doing it—*and* it's not easy. So set yourself up for success with small changes, baby steps, one brick at a time. And when you fall back into old habits (as you will), drop anchor, acknowledge the hurt, and hold yourself kindly.

PART THREE

Revitalize

19   The Stage Show of Life

I once heard a comedian say to a noisy heckler, "Two hundred million sperm—and *you* had to be the one that got through!" When we think about it in these terms—that only one out of two hundred million sperm will successfully fertilize the egg—we realize we're pretty lucky to be alive. When you consider the chain of events that had to take place in order for you to be here—how your mother had to meet your father, and how their mothers and fathers had to meet each other, and so on, back to the dawn of life—it's almost miraculous that you exist at all. In other words, we're privileged to be alive.

A "privilege" means an advantage granted to a particular person or group, and an "advantage" is a condition or circumstance that puts us in a favorable position or provides us with a valuable opportunity. Each of us is a member of a particular group that scientists refer to as *Homo sapiens*, and the fact that we're alive, when so many of our species are dead, puts us in a favorable position. It gives us a valuable opportunity to connect, care, and contribute, and to love, learn, and grow. To treat life as a privilege means to seize that opportunity—to appreciate, embrace, and savor it. I mentioned earlier that when a loss involves death, many experience a sense of doom or foreboding afterward. We become acutely aware of the inevitability of death for each and every one of us. Often this triggers anxiety, vulnerability, or insecurity. But if we explore those thoughts and feelings rather than pushing them away, we'll discover they're telling us something important; they remind us that we're all vulnerable, but also that life is precious. We never know how long we have left, so we need to make the most of the time we have. How do we actually do that? Well, if you've been applying the principles in this book you're already well on the way.

Consider the idea that life is like a stage show. All your thoughts, emotions, memories, sensations, and urges, along with everything you can see, hear, touch, taste, and smell are onstage. You can zoom in to see the details or zoom out to take in the big picture; dim the lights on one area or shine a spotlight on another. We don't have a good word for this. I call it either the "observing self" or the "part of you that notices." You've been using this for every mindfulness exercise throughout this book: noticing your thoughts, feelings, and body, as well as noticing your actions and the world around you. It's always available, and you can utilize it anytime to illuminate the aspects of the ever-changing stage show that you wish to explore. At times, the stage seems full of pleasure and joy, but at others, it's crowded with hurt and misery.

When life hits us hard, the spotlight falls on our pain and the rest of the stage darkens: it seems there's nothing to life but our suffering. But suppose we illuminate *all* of the stage. What happens if we notice *both* our pain *and* all the life around it? What if, from that space of expansive awareness, we could notice the ways in which life is *not* lacking or damaged? What if we could discover something very precious—some hidden treasure that gives us a sense of fulfillment, even in the midst of our great pain?

Of course, our minds respond, *While I have this problem/loss to deal with, nothing else matters, Without XYZ, my life is empty/meaningless,* or *I don't care about anything else.* If we get hooked by these thoughts, we'll get lost in the smog. But if we want relief from this smog, we can drop anchor and get present; we can unhook from those thoughts, cultivate awareness, and notice the *whole* of our life, not just the pain.

What might happen if you noticed everything that most of us take for granted—and not only notice them, but *appreciate, savor,* and *treasure* them? What if you, in this moment, treasured your breathing, eyesight, hearing, or the use of your arms and legs? What if you treasured your next encounter with friends, family, or neighbors? Have you ever taken a walk and celebrated the beauty around you? Have you ever breathed in the air and rejoiced in its freshness? Have you ever relished the warmth of an open fire or a comfortable bed? Have you ever savored a home-cooked meal, delighted in freshly baked bread, or loved every minute of a long hot shower? Have you ever found joy in a hug, a kiss, a book, a movie, a sunset, a flower, a child, or a pet?

Now your mind might be saying, *That's all very well, Russ, but what about people who are stuck in truly horrific circumstances? Surely this isn't relevant to them.*

My answer is: first things first. When we're hurting, we need first to drop anchor and hold ourselves kindly. Next, we need to take a stand: if we can't or won't leave, then we change what can be changed, accept what can't be changed, and live by our values. If we've done all that and the situation remains horrific, then, yes, it'll likely be very hard to find anything to appreciate, savor, or treasure—but it won't be impossible.

In his autobiography *Long Walk to Freedom*, Nelson Mandela describes how, during his long imprisonment on Robben Island, he savored his early morning marches to the quarry and appreciated the fresh sea breeze and the beautiful wildlife. Or take the case of Primo Levi, an Italian Jew, who was sent to Auschwitz for the last year of World War II. In his moving book, *If This Is a Man*, Levi describes how he endured daily backbreaking labor in the freezing Polish winter, wearing only the thinnest of clothes. But when spring appeared, he was able to truly savor the warmth of the sun. Finally, consider Victor Frankl, another Jewish prisoner in Auschwitz. In his book *Man's Search for Meaning*, he reveals how, even in the midst of all that horror, he was still able to treasure sweet memories of his wife, from their life together before the atrocities started.

Notice I'm *not* suggesting we distract ourselves or pretend the loss never happened. I'm *not* proposing that we think positively and tell ourselves that this is all for the best. And I'm definitely *not* claiming this is going to get rid of your pain and make you feel happy!

What I *am* suggesting is simply this: Let's bring up the lights on the *whole* stage show. Let's acknowledge all the difficulties, acknowledge all the painful thoughts and feelings—*and* also acknowledge the pleasures and wonders life gives us. Let's appreciate the privilege of simply being alive to witness this amazing stage show—and find something within it that we can treasure.

Of course, this is much easier said than done. Why? Because, by default, the mind focuses on what we *don't* have, on what's *not good enough,* on what needs to be fixed, solved, or changed before we can appreciate life. This means that when someone starts talking about appreciating what we have, our minds may become cynical. So if your mind protests, please treat it as if it's a loud voice in the far corner of a café: let it have its say, but don't get caught up in it or sucked into any kind of argument. Instead let's consider this: how *can* we appreciate what we have?

The Art of Appreciation

It's actually quite simple to develop appreciation for the things we have. All we need to do is pay attention in a particular way: with openness and curiosity. Let's try it now. As you read this sentence, notice how your eyes scan the page; notice how they move from word to word without any conscious effort on your part; how they go at just the right speed for you to take in the information.

Now imagine how difficult life would be if you lost your eyesight. How much would you miss out on? Imagine if you could no longer read books, watch movies, discern the facial expressions of your loved ones, check out your reflection in a mirror, watch a sunset, or drive a car.

Five Things

When you reach the end of this paragraph, stop reading for a few seconds, look around, and notice—and I mean *really notice*—five things you can see. Linger on each item for several seconds, noticing its shape, color, and texture, as if you are a curious child who has never seen anything like it. Notice any patterns or markings on the surface of these objects. Notice how the light reflects off them or the shadows they cast. Notice their contours, outlines, and whether they are moving or still. Be open to the experience to discover something new, even if your mind insists it will be boring.

Once you have finished, take a moment to consider just how much your eyes add to your life; consider what the gift of vision affords you. What would life be like if you were blind? How much would you miss out on?

This brief exercise brings together two important mindfulness skills: "engaging" and "savoring." As we pay attention with openness and curiosity, we *engage* in what we're doing; in other words, we become deeply involved in our experience. And as we truly appreciate our eyes and cherish the very miracle of vision itself, this gives rise to a sense of gratitude and fulfillment; in other words, we *savor* the experience.

Appreciation

Appreciating Your Hands

Now as you continue reading, notice how your hands effortlessly hold this book. When you get to the end of this paragraph, pick up the book, turn it upside down, flip it gently into the air, and catch it. Spend a good minute or so playing with the book in different ways. Toss it from hand to hand, or flick through all the pages, or raise it up high and let it drop, catching it before it hits the ground. As you do these things, pay attention to the movements of your hands. Be curious about your hands: notice how they know exactly what to do; how the fingers and thumbs work so smoothly together. And be open to the experience; be open to learning from it, even if you really don't want to do it.

So, how amazing are your hands? How difficult would life be if you didn't have them? When you reach the end of this paragraph, use your hands to do something pleasant for yourself—gently stroke your scalp, massage your temples, rub your eyelids, or massage a shoulder. Do this for a minute or so, slowly and gently, and again bring that childlike curiosity and openness to the process. Notice how your hands move, the sensations they generate, and the way your body responds.

Once you've done this, consider how much your hands contribute to your life and how much they enable you to do. Now try another exercise, which focuses on the breath.

Appreciating Your Breath

Now as you continue reading, slow your breathing. Take a few slow, deep breaths and let your shoulders drop. As you appreciate the simple pleasure of breathing, reflect on the role your lungs play in your life. Consider how much you rely on them. Consider how much they contribute to your well-being. Millions of people all have heart and lung diseases that make breathing very difficult—and if you've ever had asthma or pneumonia, you know just how difficult and scary that can be. Maybe you've visited someone in a hospital or a nursing home who was suffering from severe heart or lung disease; their lungs would fill with fluid and the only way they could breathe was by inhaling oxygen through a mask. Imagine if that person were you. Imagine being in that situation and looking back over your life, remembering when your lungs functioned well and how much easier your life was then. How much do we rely on our lungs and on our breath—and how often do we take them for granted? Can you, just for a moment, notice your lungs in action and notice the breath flowing rhythmically—in and out—and savor the experience?

If we take the time throughout the day to slow down and appreciate what we have, we develop a greater sense of contentment. We can do this anytime, anyplace: we simply take a few seconds to notice, with openness and curiosity, something we can see, hear, touch, taste, or smell: perhaps the smile on the face of a loved one, or motes of dust dancing in a beam of sunlight, or the sensation of breath moving in and out of our lungs, or the sound of a child laughing, or the smell of brewing coffee, or the taste of butter on toast.

Now I'm not suggesting for a moment that this will solve all your problems. Nor am I asking you to pretend that everything in your life is hunky-dory and that you have no needs, wants, and desires. The purpose of this practice is simply to increase our sense of fulfillment. "Finding the treasure" is a radically different psychological state to our default mindset of lack and discontentment.

So the next time you drink some water, why not slow down a little and savor the first sip? Swill it once or twice around your mouth and notice how it instantly eases the dryness.

And the next time you're out walking, why not take a few moments to notice the movement of your legs? Become aware of their rhythm, strength, and coordination, and appreciate how they move you around.

And next time you eat a delicious meal, why not savor the first mouthful? Marvel at how your tongue is able to taste the food, and how your teeth are able to chew, and how your throat is able to swallow.

We all tend to take life for granted, but it doesn't have to be that way. We don't have to wait until we're almost dying of thirst to appreciate the simple pleasure of drinking water. We don't have to wait until our legs stop working to appreciate how they carry us around. We don't have to wait until our eyes and ears fail to appreciate the gifts of vision and hearing. We can appreciate all these treasures, here and now.

20   The Full Experience

Suppose you are in a lovely, cool, air-conditioned hotel room. You look out through the windows and gasp in admiration at a pristine white beach and the clear blue ocean, as far as the eye can see. The waves sparkle in the sunlight and palm trees sway gently in the breeze. It's a truly spectacular view. But…you cannot hear the pounding of the waves, you cannot feel the sunlight on your face, you cannot feel the breeze tousling your hair, and you cannot breathe and smell the fresh sea air. This is what it's like to be "half present." You take in some of your experience, but you miss out on much of it.

Now suppose you leave your room and step out onto the balcony. Instantly, you feel more alive. You can feel the kiss of sunlight on your skin, the wind gently tousling your hair, and the fresh salty air filling your lungs. This is what it's like to be fully present, to engage in life as it is in this moment and soak up its richness, to drink it in and savor it. In the earlier sections of this book, we looked at mindfulness mainly as a means to reduce suffering: dropping anchor, making room for painful emotions, unhooking from difficult thoughts, and so on. We'll now explore a different aspect of mindfulness: using it to fully engage in life.

Moments of Engagement

Moments of engagement are natural. When we first meet someone we admire or find attractive, we are likely to be very engaged: we give them our full attention and hang on their every word. When we say someone has a "strong presence" or that we find them "engaging," we mean that they readily and naturally attract our attention. But what of those friends, family members, and colleagues that we see all the time: how often do we take them for granted or only half-listen to them? We may even complain about how hard it is to stay present when they "go on about things"; we may label them as "boring."

Similarly, when we taste the first mouthful of a delicious meal, smell a delightful new fragrance, or set eyes upon a rainbow, we naturally, easily give it our full attention—but very quickly, we start to take it for granted.

Let's create some moments of engagement right now. In the next exercise, do each instruction for five to ten seconds before moving on.

Mindfulness of Sounds

First, "open your ears" and simply notice what you can hear.

Notice any sounds coming from you (e.g., your body moving in your chair or your breathing).

Now "stretch out your ears" to notice the sounds nearby.

Gradually expand your hearing range until you can hear the most distant sounds possible. Can you hear the sounds of the weather or distant traffic?

Sit still in the midst of all this sound and notice the different layers: the vibrations, pulsations, and rhythms.

Notice the sounds that stop and the new ones that start. See if you can notice a continuous sound—an electrical hum or a fan whirring—and listen to it as if it's a piece of wondrous music. Notice the pitch, the volume, and the timbre.

Stay with this and notice how it's not just one sound. Notice the layers within layers, rhythms within rhythms, and cycles within cycles.

Now notice the difference between the sounds you hear and the words and pictures that your mind tries to attach to them.

How did you do? Were you able to stay fully present with the sounds, or did your mind pull you away? Most of us experience the latter. Did your mind distract you with thoughts like *This is boring, I can't do it, I don't really need to do this,* or *What's for dinner?* Did it create images of the sounds—of people, cars, birds, or the weather? Perhaps your mind had you analyzing the sounds (*What's making that noise?*) or identifying and labeling them (*That's a truck*). Maybe it just pulled you back to your loss: got you worrying about your problems, dwelling on how bad you feel, or wondering how this exercise could possibly help you. Whatever your mind did, it's quite okay; just notice that reaction and let it be.

Lisa and the Frogs

"I can't stand it," said Lisa. "If I have to listen to those damned frogs one more night, I'll go crazy!" A week earlier, Lisa had moved into a lovely new house. Unfortunately, her next-door neighbor had a large pond, which was home to a family of exceedingly loud frogs. As Lisa described it, the frogs made a noise like two blocks of wood banging together, and they made it all night long. The noise was intensely irritating and kept her awake for hours. She'd tried three different types of earplugs, all to no avail, and she confessed—very guiltily—that she'd even thought about poisoning the frogs.

I took her through the mindfulness of sounds exercise, and near the end of it, I asked her to fix her attention on the somewhat irritating sound of a lawn mower, whirring loudly across the road from my office. I asked her to be fully present with the sound, let her mind chatter away in the background, and focus her attention on the sound itself, noticing, with great curiosity, all the different elements involved—the rhythms, vibrations, high notes, low notes, changes in pitch and volume—as if she were listening to the voice of a fabulous singer. Afterward she reported that the noise quickly shifted from being annoying to rather interesting. She was amazed that she'd heard the sound of a lawnmower hundreds of times, but she'd never realized it was so complex. I asked her to practice this exercise in bed at night, to listen mindfully to the croaking frogs next door. A week later, she told me, with a huge grin, that she had practiced the exercise every night, and she now enjoyed the sound of the frogs—she found it soothing and relaxing, and it actually helped her drift off to sleep!

Exercises like this don't always have such dramatic results, especially when we're new to them and our mindfulness skills are relatively undeveloped. Plus staying present is hard to do, because our mind has so many clever ways of distracting us. So if we want to get good at this, we just need to practice. Here are two quick and simple exercises you could easily do each day.

Mindfulness

Mindfulness of People

Each day pick one person and notice their face as if you've never seen it before: the color of their eyes, teeth, and hair, the pattern of the wrinkles in their skin, and the manner in which they talk. Notice how they move and walk, their facial expressions, body language, and tone of voice. See if you can read their emotions and tune in to what they're feeling. When they talk to you, pay attention as if they are the most fascinating speaker you've ever heard and you've paid a million dollars for the privilege of listening. (Tip: Choose the person the night before and then remind yourself who it is in the morning. This way, you're more likely to remember.) Important: notice what happens as a result of this more mindful interaction.

Mindfulness of Pleasure

Every day pick a simple, pleasurable activity—ideally one that you often take for granted or do on autopilot—and see if you can extract every last sensation of pleasure out of it. This might be hugging a loved one, stroking your cat, walking your dog, playing with your kids, drinking a cool glass of water or a warm cup of tea, eating your lunch or dinner, listening to your favorite music, having a hot bath or shower, walking in the park—you name it. (Note: Don't try this with activities that require you to get lost in your thoughts, such as reading, Sudoku, chess, or crossword puzzles.) As you do this activity, use your five senses to be fully present: notice what you can see, hear, touch, taste, and smell, and savor every aspect of it.

Of course, there are an infinite number of practices that can help us develop the capacity to engage in and savor our experience. Why not invent some of your own? All you need to do is pick something—an object, activity, or event—and give it your full, open, curious attention. Take in all the details through your five senses—and at the same time, acknowledge how it contributes to your life.

Stay alert for that old Not Good Enough Story, which always lurks in the background. If it hooks us, it's like a high-speed shuttle to hell. One moment we're appreciating life here and now; the next we're deep in the bowels of the earth. Luckily, though, there's also a shuttle to heaven. As we unhook from unhelpful stories, make room for our difficult feelings, and anchor ourselves firmly in the present, we ascend from the depths and come into the light. And when we go one step further and consciously appreciate what we have, we discover that our reality is transformed. Our pain does not disappear, but it no longer dominates our attention; so, as well as acknowledging what we have lost, we can notice and appreciate what we have.

21   Joy and Sorrow

When my client Chloe was diagnosed with breast cancer, she joined a so-called "support group." She'd hoped to find a compassionate, self-aware community that could realistically acknowledge how painful, scary, and difficult cancer is, while also providing support and genuine encouragement. What she found instead was, in her words, "a bunch of positive-thinking fanatics." They didn't acknowledge Chloe's pain and fear, but told her to think positively—to see her cancer as a "gift." They said she should consider herself lucky because this illness gave her a chance to "wake up" and appreciate her life, a chance to learn, grow, and love more fully.

I'm all for learning, growing, and loving more fully, and this whole book is about waking up and appreciating life. But it's a big leap from that to seeing your cancer as a gift or considering yourself lucky to have it. Replace the word "cancer" with "your child's death," "your house destroyed by fire," "sexual assault," "living in a refugee camp," or "losing your limbs." How callous to call these experiences "gifts" and to tell people they're "lucky"! That's the very opposite of a caring and compassionate response. If something terrible happens, by all means let's learn and grow from it, but let's not pretend that it's wonderful or we're lucky to have it.

Yet, occasionally you'll meet or hear of someone who says that their illness, injury, or near-death experience was the "best thing that ever happened" to them because it transformed their life in such a positive way. I've met a couple of these folks, and I've read about others—the genuine ones are truly inspiring. These people, however, are extremely rare, and most of us will never see things the same way. So why not be honest with ourselves?

When bad things happen, let's acknowledge our pain and be kind to ourselves. Only then can we consider how we might learn or grow from the experience.

So, if you *have* acknowledged your pain, responded with kindness, and done what you can to improve the situation, then it may *now* be time to consider several questions. Given that this huge loss *has* happened, it may be useful to ask yourself:

- *How can I learn or grow from this experience?*

- *What personal qualities could I develop?*

- *What practical skills might I learn or improve?*

- *What strengths can I develop?*

- *What relationships can I deepen?*

Every major loss invites us to grow. We don't *want* that invitation, but if we turn it down, our life is sure to get worse. So how about we accept it and make the most of it? Let's use it to develop mindfulness and self-compassion, to get in touch with our values and act with purpose.

Part of the privilege of life is that we *do* have the opportunity to learn and grow, and we can make use of this opportunity anytime, anyplace, right up until we die. So let's be curious: How can we deepen our life in response to distress? Can we perhaps develop more patience or courage? Or compassion, persistence, or forgiveness?

Have you heard the saying, "When the student is ready, the teacher appears"? I once considered it "New Age" claptrap, and thought it meant that as soon as you were ready for the secret of enlightenment, some guru would magically appear out of thin air. But now I interpret it very differently: if we're willing to learn, we can do so from literally anything life dishes up. No matter how painful or scary, we can always learn something useful from it.

Now suppose I say to you, "I've got this gadget," and I pull out a little silver box with a bright red button on top. "This device is amazing," I continue. "Just press this red button and all your fear, anger, guilt, loneliness, and sadness will disappear—and painful memories too. In fact, you'll never experience pain ever again. There's only one side effect. When you press that button, you won't care about anyone or anything. You won't care about your friends, partner, or family; you won't care if they're happy or sad, if they live or die. You won't care about your career, your house, your neighborhood, your country, the planet; you won't care about anything that happens, ever. You'll have no goals, no desires, no wishes. Your life will lack any sense of meaning or purpose, because you care about absolutely nothing. But hey—you'll have no more pain."

Would you press that button?

This is what life gives us. If we care about anyone or anything, then sooner or later we'll encounter a gap between what we want and what we've got—and the bigger that gap, the greater our pain. *Those things that truly matter also hurt.*

So can we make room for those painful feelings and see them as a valuable part of us? Can we appreciate that they tell us something important: we are alive, we have a heart, and we truly care?

Can we see our pain as a bridge to the hearts of others, a bridge that spans our differences and unites us in the commonality of human suffering? Only when we know what it's like to hurt can we relate well to others who are suffering; only then will we understand the true meaning of empathy. Can we appreciate how pain helps us to build rich relationships, to *connect* with the pain of others, to actively *care* about them, and to willingly *contribute* kindness when they're hurting?

Our emotions are as much a part of us as our arms and our legs, so do we really have to avoid, escape, or fight them? When our arms and legs are injured, we experience pain—but we don't get into a fight with our limbs because of it, or wish we could go through life without them. We appreciate what they contribute to our life.

Now let's consider the part of us that cares. What if we could truly treasure this part and be grateful for all it affords us in life? Yes, if we didn't care, we'd have no pain, but we'd also have no joy, love, or laughter. We'd go through life like zombies; everything would be pointless or meaningless. There'd be no disappointment or frustration, but there would also be no contentment or satisfaction. Our capacity to care enables us to live a life of purpose: to build rich relationships, motivate ourselves, find life's treasures, and enjoy them. So can we be grateful for caring, even though it brings us so much pain?

Let's also consider our ability to *feel* emotions. Can we appreciate the brain's amazing ability to take billions of electrochemical signals from all over the body, decode and interpret them in an instant, to enable us to feel whatever we feel?

Just imagine if this system didn't work. Imagine if we felt nothing ever again. How much would we miss out on? How empty would life be?

From a mental viewpoint of self-compassion, having dropped anchor and taken a purposeful stand, can we look at these painful feelings inside our body and treat them with kindness and respect? Can we give them space, peace, and our caring attention? Can we reflect on how they remind us of what we care about? Can we let go of judging these feelings as "bad" and instead cultivate wonder that they exist at all?

I've saved this chapter to the end because this is hardest thing I suggest in this book. To tolerate pain is difficult; to accept it is much harder. But to appreciate it is the hardest challenge of all.

And yet, it is possible. The more we reflect on the privilege of human emotion—that we get to care and to feel in so many different ways—the more we can appreciate *all* our emotions. But this privilege doesn't come without a price. With passion comes pain. With caring comes loss. With wonder comes fear and dread.

The famous Lebanese author Kahlil Gibran expressed these ideas wonderfully in his amazing book of poetry, *The Prophet*. Here's an excerpt from his poem "On Joy and Sorrow":

Your joy is your sorrow unmasked.

And the selfsame well from which your laughter rises was oftentimes filled with your tears.

And how else can it be?

The deeper that sorrow carves into your being, the more joy you can contain.

Is not the cup that holds your wine the very cup that was burned in the potter's oven?

And is not the lute that soothes your spirit, the very wood that was hollowed with knives?

When you are joyous, look deep into your heart and you shall find it is only that which has given you sorrow that is giving you joy.

When you are sorrowful look again in your heart, and you shall see that in truth you are weeping for that which has been your delight.

Some of you say, "Joy is greater than sorrow," and others say, "Nay, sorrow is the greater."

But I say unto you, they are inseparable.

Together they come, and when one sits alone with you at your board, remember that the other is asleep upon your bed.

Life is a great privilege, and we are challenged to make the most of it. Can we let our values guide us, can we treat ourselves kindly, make room for both our sorrow and our joy, and engage fully in the great and ever-changing stage show of life? Yes, we can—though we will often forget to do this. But whenever we *do* remember, we have a choice. We can hold ourselves kindly, drop anchor, and take a stand. And right there, in that moment, we can find treasure; it's always there, even when life hits hard.

Appendices

A   Neutralization

Neutralizing your thoughts means putting them into a new context where you can readily recognize that they are constructs of words and pictures; this neutralizes their power, making it easier to unhook from them.

Neutralization techniques typically involve either highlighting the visual properties of thoughts (i.e., "seeing" them) or the auditory properties of thoughts (i.e., "hearing" them), or both. Remember that the purpose of unhooking is *not* to get rid of unwanted thoughts or to reduce unpleasant feelings. It's to enable you to engage fully in life instead of getting lost in or pushed around by your thoughts. When we unhook from unhelpful thoughts, we often find that they quickly "disappear" or unpleasant feelings rapidly reduce, but such outcomes are lucky bonuses, not the main aim.

Try the following techniques and be curious about what happens. Some may work really well, others not at all. If you find one or two that really help you to unhook, experiment with them over the next few weeks and see what difference they make. However, if any technique makes you feel trivialized or mocked, then do *not* use it.

Visual Neutralization Techniques

On a piece of paper, jot down several of the thoughts that most frequently hook you and distress you. For each technique below, pick one of these thoughts to work with, go step-by-step through the exercise, and be curious about and open to whatever happens.

Thoughts on Paper

Write two or three distressing thoughts on a large piece of paper.

Now hold the piece of paper in front of your face and get absorbed in those distressing thoughts for a few seconds.

Next, place the paper down on your lap, look around you, and notice what you can see, hear, touch, taste, and smell.

Notice the thoughts are still with you. Notice they haven't changed at all, and you know exactly what they are—but does their impact lessen when you rest them on your lap instead of hold them in front of your face?

Now on the paper, underneath those thoughts, draw a stick figure (or, if you have an artistic streak, some sort of cartoon character). Draw a "thought bubble" around those words, as if they are coming out of the head of your stick figure (like thought bubbles you see in comic strips). Now look at your "cartoon": does this make any difference to the way you relate to those thoughts?

Try this a few times with different thoughts and stick figures (or cartoons). Put different faces on your stick figures—smiley face, sad face, or face with big teeth or spiky hair. Draw a cat, a dog, or a flower with those very same thought bubbles coming out of it. Does this change the impact of those thoughts? Does it help you to see them as words?

Computer Screen

You can do this exercise in your imagination or on a computer. (For most people, it's more powerful on a computer.) First write (or imagine) your thought in standard black lowercase text on the computer screen, then play around with it. Change it into different colors, fonts, and sizes, and notice what effect each change makes. (Note: Bold red capitals are likely to hook most people, whereas a lowercase pale pink font is more likely to help us unhook from unhelpful thoughts.)

Then change the text back to black lowercase. This time play around with the formatting:

Space the words out, placing large gaps between them.

Run the words together with no gaps between them so they make one long word.

Run them vertically down the screen.

Then put them back together as one sentence.

How do you relate to those thoughts now? Is it easier to see that they are words? (Remember, we are not interested in whether the thoughts are true or false; we want to see them for what they are—just words.)

Karaoke Ball

Imagine your thoughts as words on a karaoke screen. Imagine a "bouncing ball" jumping from word to word across the screen. Repeat this several times.

If you like, you can even imagine yourself up on stage singing along with the words on the screen.

Changing Scenarios

Imagine your thought in a variety of different settings. Take about 5 to 10 seconds to imagine each scenario, then move on to the next one. See your thought written

- in playful colorful letters on the cover of a children's book,

- as stylish graphics on a restaurant menu,

- as icing on top of a birthday cake,

- in chalk on a blackboard,

- as a slogan on a jogger's T-shirt..

Leaves on a Stream or Clouds in the Sky

Imagine leaves gently floating down a stream or clouds gently floating through the sky. Place your thoughts on those leaves or clouds, and watch them gently float by.

Auditory Neutralization Techniques

These techniques give you more opportunities to place your thoughts in a different context. Experiment with them and notice what happens.

Silly Voices

Say your thought in a silly voice—either silently or out loud. (Out loud is often more helpful, but obviously you need to pick an appropriate time and place.) You might choose the voice of a cartoon character, movie star, sports commentator, or someone with an outrageous foreign accent. Try several different voices and notice what happens.

Slow and Fast

Say your thought—either silently or out loud—first very slowly, then at superfast speed (so you sound like a chipmunk).

Singing

Sing your thoughts—either silently or out loud—to the tune of "Happy Birthday." Then try it with a couple of different tunes.

Create Your Own Neutralization Techniques

Now invent your own neutralization techniques. Just put your thought in a new context where you can "see" it or "hear" it, or both. You might visualize your thought painted on a canvas, printed on a postcard, emblazoned on the chest of a comic book superhero, carved on the shield of a medieval knight, trailed on a banner behind an airplane, tattooed on the back of a biker, or written on the side of a zebra among all its stripes. Or you could paint it, draw it, or sculpt it. You could imagine it dancing, jumping, or playing football, or visualize it moving down a TV screen, like the credits of a movie. Alternatively, you might imagine hearing your thought being recited by a Shakespearean actor, broadcast from a radio, emanating from a robot, or sung by a rock star. You are limited only by your own creativity, so be sure to play around and have some fun.

B   Mindfulness of the Breath

This exercise is very useful for developing your mindfulness skills. (Download a free audio recording from a link in my e-book, *When Life Hits Hard: Extra Bits,* which you'll find on the Free Resources page of www .thehappinesstrap.com.) Before commencing, decide how long you'll spend on this practice—ten to twenty minutes is ideal, but you can do it for as little or as long as you wish. (It's good to use a timer.) Also, remember that occasionally people have unpleasant reactions when focusing on the breath, such as dizziness, pins and needles, or anxiety; if this happens for you, stop the exercise.

Find a quiet place free from distractions such as pets, children, and phone calls. Get into a comfortable position, ideally sitting up in a chair or on a cushion. (Lying down is okay, but you may fall asleep!) If you're sitting, straighten your back and let your shoulders drop. Then close your eyes or fix them on a spot. (It's easier to stay awake if your eyes are open.)

For the first few breaths, focus on gently emptying your lungs; ever so slowly, exhale until your lungs are completely empty. Then pause for a second, and then allow them to fill by themselves, from the bottom up.

After five or six of these breaths, allow your breathing to find its own natural pace and rhythm; there's no need to control it.

Now keep your attention on the breath. Observe it as if you were a curious child who has never encountered breathing before. As your breath flows in and out, notice the sensations you feel in your body. Notice what happens in your nostrils…in your shoulders…in your chest…in your abdomen.

With openness and curiosity, track your breath as it flows through your body; follow the trail of sensations in your nose, shoulders, chest, and abdomen.

As you do this, let your mind chatter away like a radio in the background: don't try to silence it. Simply let your mind chatter away and keep your attention on the breath.

Occasionally, your mind will hook you with thoughts and feelings. This is normal and natural—and will keep happening. Once you realize you've been hooked, gently acknowledge it. Silently say, *Hooked,* or gently nod your head and refocus on your breath.

This "hooking" will happen again and again. Each time you unhook yourself and return your attention to the breath, you're building your ability to focus. So if your mind hooks you one thousand times, then one thousand times you acknowledge it and refocus on your breathing.

As you continue, the feelings and sensations in your body will change: you may notice pleasant ones, such as relaxation, calmness, and peace, or uncomfortable ones, such as backache, frustration, or anxiety. Allow your feelings, painful or pleasant, to be as they are.

Remember, this is *not* a relaxation technique. You aren't trying to relax. It's quite all right if you feel stressed, anxious, bored, or impatient. Just allow your feelings to be as they are in this moment—without a struggle.

If a difficult feeling is present, silently name it: *Here's boredom, Here's frustration,* or *Here's anxiety.* Let it be, and keep your attention on the breath.

Continue in this way—observing the breath, acknowledging uncomfortable feelings, unhooking yourself from thoughts—until you reach the end of your allotted time.

Now stretch leisurely, engage with the world around you, and congratulate yourself on taking the time to practice this valuable life skill.

c Goal Setting

Effective goal setting is an important skill; you have to practice to get the hang of it. This method is adapted with permission from the book *The Weight Escape* by Ann Bailey, Joe Ciarrochi, and Russ Harris. You can download this worksheet from my free e-book, *When Life Hits Hard: Extra Bits,* which you'll find on the Free Resources page of www.thehappinesstrap. com.

The Five-Step Plan for Goal Setting and Committed Action

Step 1: Identify Your Guiding Values.

Identify the value or values that will underpin your course of action.

_____

_____

_____

_____

_____

Step 2: Set a SMART Goal.

It's not effective to set just any goal. Ideally, you want to set a SMART goal:

S = specific. Do not set a vague, fuzzy, or poorly defined goal like "I'll be more loving." Instead, be specific: "I'll give my partner a good long hug when I get home from work." In other words, _specify_ what actions you will take.

M = motivated by values. Make sure this goal is aligned with your chosen values.

A = adaptive. Is it wise to pursue this goal? Is it likely to make your life better?

R = realistic. Make sure the goal is realistic for the resources you have available. Resources could include time, money, physical health, social support, knowledge, and skills. If these resources are necessary but unavailable, you'll need to change to a more realistic goal. The new goal might be to find the missing resources: to save the money, develop the skills, build the social network, or improve your health.

T = time framed. Designate a specific time frame. Specify the day, date, and time—as accurately as possible—that you will take the proposed actions.

Write your SMART goal here:

_____

_____

_____

_____

_____

Step 3: Identify Benefits.

What would be the most positive outcome(s) of achieving your goal? (However, *don't* start fantasizing about how wonderful life will be after you achieve your goal; research shows that fantasizing about the future actually reduces your chances of following through!) Write the benefits below:

_____

_____

_____

_____

_____

Step 4: Identify Obstacles.

Identify potential difficulties and obstacles that might stand in your way, and indicate how you will deal with them if they arise.

- What are the possible *internal* difficulties (low motivation, self-doubt, distress, anger, hopelessness, insecurity, anxiety, etc.)?

- What are the possible *external* difficulties (lack of money, time, or skills, or personal conflicts with other people involved)?

List internal difficulties (thoughts and feelings) that might arise:

_____

_____

_____

List the ACT skills (e.g., unhooking, making room, self-compassion, dropping anchor) you will use to deal with internal difficulties:

_____

_____

_____

List external difficulties that might arise:

_____

_____

_____

Indicate how you will deal with each external difficulty you've listed above:

_____

_____

_____

Step 5: Make a Commitment.

Research shows that if you make a public commitment to your goal (i.e., state your goal to at least one other person), you are far more likely to follow through on it. If you're not willing to do this, then at the very least make a commitment to yourself. But if you really *do* want the best results, then make your commitment to somebody else you trust.

I commit to (write your values-guided SMART goal here):

_____

_____

_____

_____

_____

Now say your commitment out loud—ideally to someone else, but if not, to yourself.

Other Helpful Tips for Goal Setting

- Make a step-by-step plan: break your goal down into concrete, measurable, and time-based subgoals.

- Tell supportive people about your goal and your ongoing progress: a public declaration increases commitment.

- Reward yourself for making progress toward your goal: small rewards help push you on to major success. (A reward might be as simple as saying to yourself, *Well done! You made a start!*)

- Record your progress: keep a journal, graph, or drawing that plots your progress.

Resources

When Life Hits Hard: Extra Bits

This free e-book (PDF) contains links to free audio recordings, plus additional resources. Download it from the Free Resources page on www.thehappinesstrap.com.

Other Books by Russ Harris

The Happiness Trap: Stop Struggling, Start Living

The Happiness Trap explores how to make life richer, fuller, and more meaningful, while avoiding common "happiness traps." Based on ACT (acceptance and commitment therapy), it applies to everything from work stress and addictions, anxiety and depression, to the pressures of parenting and challenges of terminal illness. Widely used by ACT practitioners and their clients all around the world, *The Happiness Trap* has sold over one million copies, and been translated into over thirty languages.

ACT with Love

This inspiring and empowering self-help book teaches you how to apply the principles of ACT to common relationship issues, and shows how to move from conflict, struggle, and disconnection to forgiveness, acceptance, intimacy, and genuine loving.

The Confidence Gap

Do you want to do something important in your work, personal, or family life, but fear, doubt, or insecurity gets in your way? This book reveals how to overcome fear and develop genuine confidence, using the principles of ACT. Compassionate, practical, and inspiring, *The Confidence Gap* will help you identify your passions, succeed at your challenges, and create a life that is truly fulfilling.

ACT Made Simple: An Easy-to-Read Primer on Acceptance and Commitment Therapy (second edition)

This practical and entertaining textbook for psychologists, counselors, therapists, and coaches is equally useful for experienced ACT practitioners and newcomers to the approach. *ACT Made Simple* offers clear explanations of the core ACT processes, and real-world tips and solutions for rapidly and effectively implementing them in your coaching or therapy practice. Reading this book is all the training you need to begin using ACT techniques with your clients for impressive results.

Audio MP3s by Russ Harris

Mindfulness Skills: Volumes 1 and 2, available as downloadable MP3 files, cover a wide range of mindfulness exercises for personal use. You can get them via the online store on www.ACTmindfully.com.au.

"In Person" and Online ACT Training for Health Professionals

Russ Harris provides a wide range of professional ACT training for therapists, coaches, counselors, doctors, nurses, social workers, psychologists, psychiatrists, youth workers, and occupational therapists. These workshops and courses are available both "in person" and online.

- For online courses, see www.ImLearningACT.com.

- For "in person" workshops in Australia, see www.ACTmindfully .com.au.

The Happiness Trap: Online Self-Help Program

Have you tried hard to be happier and found it just wasn't that easy? If so, that's hardly surprising. Commonplace notions of happiness are misleading, inaccurate, and can actually make you miserable. So come along and learn about *happiness without all the hype*. Learn how to escape "the happiness trap" and find genuine well-being and fulfillment. This entertaining and empowering online program, written and presented by Russ Harris, is based on his international bestseller *The Happiness Trap*. To find out more, go to www.thehappinesstrap.com.

Facebook Groups

Health professionals (of any sort): Check out the "ACT Made Simple" Facebook group. Tens of thousands of health practitioners from around the world ask questions, provide answers, and share resources about anything and everything to do with the professional use of ACT in counseling, coaching, and therapy.

Personal growth/self-help: Join the "Happiness Trap Online" Facebook group. It's a private group where we can all share our struggles and explore how to use ACT with them.

Acknowledgments

First and foremost, I am deeply indebted and incredibly grateful to my partner, Natasha, for all her love and support while I was writing this book—as well as all her love and support when I was not writing the book!

Next, a planet-sized amount of thanks to Steven Hayes, the originator of ACT, for not only introducing this amazing model to the world, but also for all his help and encouragement with my books and my career. That gratitude also extends to the larger ACT community worldwide, which is always very supportive, giving, and caring.

Third, my thanks to Joe Ciarrochi and Ann Bailey for allowing me to use the goal-setting materials we created for *The Weight Escape*.

Fourth, many thanks to the Australia/New Zealand team at Exisle Publishing—especially Gareth Thomas, Anouska Jones, and Karen Gee for all their hard work, care, and attention.

And last but not least, truckloads of thanks to the New Harbinger team, especially Jean Blomquist for a superb editing job, and Clancy Drake, Tesilya Hanauer, and Catharine Meyers for supporting and nurturing this new edition.

Russ Harris is a medical practitioner, psychotherapist, and best-selling author of *The Happiness Trap*—which has now been translated into thirty languages and sold more than one million copies. Russ is one of the world's leading authorities on acceptance and commitment therapy (ACT), and has trained over 50,000 health practitioners in the approach. In 2015, he wrote an ACT protocol for the World Health Organization (WHO) to use in refugee camps—and their research shows this brief intervention leads to significant improvements in post-traumatic stress disorder (PTSD) and depression.

MORE BOOKS from
NEW HARBINGER PUBLICATIONS

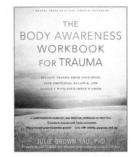
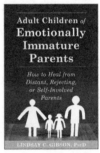